CW00486642

Copyright 2023 Sue Clancy

All Rights Reserved

ISBN: 9798371489081

ACKNOWLEDGEMENTS

My heartfelt thanks to everyone who has encouraged me

or shown any interest in this book.

But especially my three wonderful daughters.

My eight lovable grandchildren.

And of course, all of the brave clients that I have had the pleasure of working with.

RADICAL SELF LOVE

healing for the inner child

Sue Clancy

"Always remember that you are braver
than you believe, stronger than you seem,

smarter than you think, and twice as
beautiful as you'd ever imagined.

Yesterday I was clever, so I wanted to
change the world.

Today I am wise, so I am changing myself."

Rumi (1207-1273)

INTRODUCTION

If I were to ask you about what kind of voices you hear in your head? You might say, "I have terrible voices in my head; they sound judgmental, dishonest, envious and extremely critical, and sometimes even hateful. I try to ignore them, but there are times when I feel as if I am going mad."

If you're tired of these voices and their messages, maybe you're ready to do something different. There is a way to change this damaging, negative inner self talk, to understand where they come from, why they exist, and what you can do with them.

My experiences have brought me to this place, where I can share with you what I have learned over the past thirty-seven years and not only from information and theory, but perhaps more importantly, what I have learned about my own self-defeating patterns.

From this perspective, I believe that I have a deeper understanding of internal negative self-talk and its soul-destroying impact. This book is primarily about the internal negative voices that are, to varying degrees, a part of everyone's psychological makeup.

Also that this is a helpful process that has worked for many of my clients as well as for myself, and It is not made up of vague ideas or suggestions to be nicer to yourself. This way is not about simply meditating, even though meditation can certainly be helpful in soothing distress and anxiety.

In simple terms, my theory is that if we really begin to listen to what our voices are saying, maybe we can learn to understand ourselves better because these aspects of us are not always speaking the truth. They may be telling lies or misleading us for very specific reasons.

Understanding something has always been the first step toward change, and when we get to the point of wanting to change, we are faced with a difficult choice. If we want to flourish and grow instead of remaining emotionally stunted and trapped in repeating old patterns that take us around and around on the same old merry-go-round. We must undo the emotional pain we cause ourselves by believing that we are bad, unlovable, alone, or unloved.

If you are ready for this change, then you are in the right place. You may have low self-esteem. You may have noticed that your self-talk is unhelpful. You may also never have paid attention to the frequency or the severity, but you do know that there is an inner voice and that it is not on your side.

Welcome to you.

It is my hope that this book is written with enough truth and insight for you to begin to understand what it is that causes your suffering. Because I think the most important job that a self-help book has to do is: to give a clear understanding of the problem, some background to the theory of the problem, and, of course, an easy-to-follow process that makes change possible.

PS. I have given some thought to using pronouns, so I have made a decision to use him, her, and they. They will be interchangeable, each one in different paragraphs and there is no underlying decision for the use of any one in particular. Please just switch to whichever pronoun fits for you; your brain will easily adjust, I think. This is so that no one is excluded from this work. Thanks for your understanding.

One

About Change.

"If you can't fly then run.

If you can't run then walk.

If you can't walk then crawl.

But whatever you do you have to keep moving forward."

Matin Luther King Jr. (1929-1968)

Change is a process.

Change is mostly a series of steps, preferably repeated continuously for better results. Us humans tend to think of change as a one-off event, something that happens once, and then change is achieved.

But had we looked at the 'event' from a different perspective, we would see that the beginning is just that, a beginning, and in fact, is made up of many new beginnings each day.

An example is when we want to lose weight, we may stop eating the things that are fattening, or we may go to the gym or count calories. But when we give up after a short time with very little change, we believe that we have failed and that the change we wanted should have been achieved in one single action. That action is we stopped eating crap, and therefore we have changed, and the desired effect (weight loss) should now have happened. But it didn't happen as we wanted, and we fell out of love with the idea that we wanted to change something, because it is hard to change.

If we view change as a process and not an event, we can start to make progress, and we can turn down the expectations that we should get everything right as soon as we try something new.

Because it isn't like that, and we can understand this more through understanding neuro-physics and the findings that tell us, about how the brain is wired to stay in the same physical grooves, which are like super highways and we make use of them by using the exact same thoughts repetitively.

Our brain prefers to perform routine tasks, because staying in the same routine is supposedly easier. However, it is easy enough to alter our course and take different actions by acting differently. Although it may seem self-evident, it really is that straightforward, and we may alter the direction we are now travelling, into a new pathway more easily than we supposed.

.Change needs to be committed to in every new moment of every day. We can say to ourselves, "Today I will carry on, and I will do again today what I did yesterday," then we can see that there is a process to everything and that this is exactly in line with how all life flows. It is our views and our belief system that causes us to distort the way the world really is and not how our 'lazy' thinking wants it to be.

Change is difficult

We also believe that change is too hard, and when we believe that, we give up too easily. We believe that we have no willpower and that we are weak and a failure, and of course, our negative voices are very good at jumping in and confirming that we are weak and probably a complete failure at almost everything we attempt to accomplish. This voice may also drag up all the other times that we have appeared to fail, even things that we may have previously resolved, understood, or even forgotten about those difficult incidents from our past.

The inner voice seems as if it will never forget about any of our mistakes, anything we may have said that caused us to feel stupid, anything that we have done that caused us embarrassment. It's all waiting inside our negative thought patterns to be brought into our consciousness at just the right time, the 'right' time being exactly the 'wrong' time!

Such as when we are feeling ill, and our body is weaker than usual; in the middle of the night when sleep escapes us; when we have made a mistake and done something that we wish we hadn't; when we have an important appointment, interview, performance; or in fact, any time when we want to appear as our best selves.

Our negative inner voices are always ready to reinforce our insecurities, to affirm our internal beliefs about our capacity for failure and to reinforce our sense of uselessness.

Most people see change as difficult to achieve or see it as something that is too risky, and with these thoughts, we are deterred from making changes, and we avoid the effort needed or become averse to the risks involved in actual change. Statistics tell us that at least 80% of the population is actually afraid of change.

As we hold onto these thoughts of the difficulty in making changes, we are then joined by the negative voice that seems keen to impress upon us the dangers that change can bring and the effort needed to even start to change something in our lives. We may desire this change with every fibre of our body, but the belief is that we are incapable of it, and the inner voice readily agrees.

Change is inevitable

Change is also inevitable; it is the one constant thing that we can rely on. Everything changes regularly, every day. As we wake up in the morning, there is nothing about us that is the same as yesterday. Our cells have grown and mutated, all of our bodily functions have progressed a fraction, and we are one day older, yet this is a long and inevitable process, and so we don't notice it happening daily. When we do notice it, we do it from the position of hindsight; we look back to the past year and see our changes, and we look back over a decade and see even more change. Maybe we believe that change is just the intervention of fate, some believe change is God given, accidental, or down to someone else's actions, depending on our personal belief system. We may play the victim's role and bemoan fates intervention in our lives.

If we were somehow suddenly freed from negative judgement and were to look back at our lives, we may see that the changes we have made over time have sometimes been good. Some of the changes, we would see that we had a hand in them, that we made things happen of our own volition and our will. Some changes we would like, and we would see had benefitted us over time. If we really had managed to let go of the judgment and were truly able to look back without its interference, then we might be able to see our lives with more compassion and to understand that we are complicated creatures, made more complicated by the judgemental voices that live inside our minds and can always be relied upon to turn a problem into a complete disaster

But more understanding is needed to discover where these voices originate from and how they exist in your mind. Why do you listen to them? Why do you think that they are in charge of you? Your freedom comes from the liberation from your own negative feedback. You then become the master of your own destiny. Where you can decide what your future is going to be, how you will respond to others, which information you will base your actions on and how you will make the choices that will benefit you, and not harm you. You will have a newfound internal strength to make your own uncontaminated decisions about your life and this is a valuable asset to have.

TWO

Be careful of your thoughts.

Be careful of your thoughts for your thoughts
become your words.

Be careful of your words for your words
become your actions.

Be careful of your actions for your actions
become your habits.

Be careful of your habits for your habits
become your character.

Be careful of your character for your
character becomes your destiny.

We all have our own thoughts, some of them we share, and some remain private. Everyone thinks, and everyone has thoughts. However, not everyone has the same thoughts or even the same kind of thoughts or way of thinking.

These are some of the many different ways of how the mind can get stuck into patterns of thinking that can interfere with our lives. The mind loves shortcuts and is very fond of lazy thinking. In fact, most of these examples are of the mind rushing down those well-worn grooves and failing to think about actions on a deeper level.

1)   **Unconscious thoughts.** When we are not thinking of anything specific, these thoughts are what we sometimes call daydreaming. Some people use this process more than others, and it can be very enjoyable to them and, in fact, can be used as a distraction. They can be useful and soothing or unhelpful and avoidant. This thinking is very common, and most people do this regularly.

2)   **Conscious thought.** Where we actively become involved in the thinking process. It may start as unconscious, but we may get interested in a particular aspect of thought, and we pursue these thoughts about things, whether this is in a destructive way or a positive one; either way, we appear to be intentionally thinking.   Often we mull over problems in this way, and then this thinking becomes emotional, and our

feelings too can get involved, and it becomes more difficult to sort out our thoughts from our emotional selves. But I think it's true to say that our feelings are always unconsciously involved in our logical mind process to some extent.

3) **Intellectual and focused thinking** (Analytical thinking). This way of thinking involves planning, solving, inventive, literary, and scholarly direction. For the most part, it is separated from emotional contamination, a bit like Dr. Spock from Star Trek. This way of using our thought process is usually not available to everyone; it needs a high IQ and a creative mind, follows logical steps, and is often focused on particular problems to solve. The drawback of this focused thought process is that sometimes the exclusion of emotions leaves out a great deal of information that could inform the thinking, making it richer and having more depth. But intellectual thinking does not often value emotions, and fails to see its worth, and appears afraid that feelings will destroy the ability to remain cognitive.

4) **Obsessional thinking.** This does exactly what it says. This is the kind of mind that easily gets tangled up in loops of obsession. Getting one particular thought and becoming obsessed with this one thought, over and over, like the mind is on a loop. This thinking can be very disturbing to

the individual and can also get into a double whammy of obsessional thoughts that are particularly invasive and dark. This person seems to have no tools and no skills to come away from this thinking and replace it with more positive, logical thinking or move into a more hopeful state of mind where the future looks brighter instead of darker and hopeless. This process is driven by the desire to keep life safe and to try to keep emotions that are difficult suppressed.

5) **Concrete thinking** is when people jump to conclusions. Only seeing what is in front of them and this becomes their absolute truth, with no further thoughts about that which they have already accepted as reality. Once committed to a truth, these people will often defend their views as if any other reality would threaten their own. This process is very much driven by fear.

6) **Black and white thinking.** When we are thinking in concrete terms and using words like always, never, completely, and perfectly, reality is then reduced to all or nothing, and life has no grey areas, and the possibility for change seems very distant. Like going from low to high, there are no steps in between, and so, no possibility of ever achieving anything as a process. It is either this or that, and it is again run by fear.

Fear of getting things wrong, fear of appearing stupid, the determination to be right because right seems safer.

7) **Blaming thought.** We blame someone else for our mistakes, problems, or setbacks. We blame ourselves and can be hard and unforgiving towards ourselves. Or we blame certain situations that have caused us to go wrong, not get what we think we need, or generally have our life disrupted. We then take no responsibility for our own part in our lives; we avoid taking responsibility as it seems too shaming and difficult.

8) **Catastrophizing** is the building up of events and the possible consequences to us or others; these events may seem insufferable or particularly awful. We often tell ourselves that we couldn't exist anymore if these horrible things were to happen in our lives. It is a form of hopeless thinking run on feelings of fear and desperation.

9) **Minimising** is when we make our shortcomings larger or enlarge someone else's gifts or accomplishments whilst making our own achievements very small and insignificant. We are always the lesser person or have the smallest assets or achievements compared to others, and 'others' seem to be the exaggerated 'everyone' These patterns are rooted in a lack of self-esteem.

10) **Fortune Telling** happens when we assume that we know the outcome of something and we jump to conclusions, which are usually bad news for us. But we have no facts to back it up and no reality to compare the event against. These thoughts seem to be run by fear and the need to know in order to feel safe.

11) **Mindreading** is where we predict and believe that we really know what another person is thinking without checking it out with them. These thoughts are usually negative; we assume that others think bad of us, and we continue to act as if this is true. Fear of being disliked or not being approved of.

12) **Selective interpretation** is that we only choose to believe those statements which fit with our own experience and expectations. So we take information and use it to fit into only our own reality. It seems safer to cling to the known information, even when there is evidence that our perception is not true,

13) **Should & Ought**. We frequently feel that the verbs "should" and "ought" refer to our own actions but also to the actions and reactions of others. They ought to respect me; thus, they should behave in this manner. These feelings and words are frequently a reaction to perceived wrongs that we feel others have done to us. They

frequently include expectations of others and omit any information that would alter the perception of what is appropriate behaviour on the part of others. Thinking about what we "should" be doing, "could have done," or "must do" might cause us serious harm. The dread of making mistakes or otherwise being "wrong" fuels this way of thinking and acts like a straight jacket for the mind.

All of these thought processes are dysfunctional ways of thinking, and it is helpful for us to understand these more or less unconscious patterns that we use as a kind of shorthand way of thinking but also a way of protecting ourselves. It can be really helpful to know which patterns of thoughts we most easily slip into and recognise the ones that we use most frequently.

When we notice these patterns of thinking about life, ourselves, and others, we have a key to changing the way we think, which will have an impact on the way we perceive life and the other people in our lives. This then leads to healthier thought patterns, less judgement of ourselves, and others, therefore more happiness. It is a good place to start the 'clean up' operation of our minds many processes and to avoid our thoughts using those well worn 'grooves' in the brain.

Three

Listen to your inner voice.

The quieter you become, the more you are able
to hear.

Rumi (1207-1273)

The difference between thoughts and voices'

I have paid a lot of attention to the difference between thoughts and inner voices, researching what others have said about the differences. Studies have noticed that there doesn't seem to be any difference; the difference seems to be in the way people describe what they hear. These studies are done with people who do not have any history of mental illness and that will report either 'hearing' a voice inside or 'thinking' a voice inside, and there being very little difference between the two things in the way they are reported. It seems that there is mainly a difference in the way different people use language.

Hearing voices is not something that most people want to admit to, sometimes because of the connection with the mental illness known as schizophrenia. One of the main symptoms of this illness is hearing voices, usually voices that sound as if they are outside the mind and often very destructive voices that tell the sufferer to harm themselves or others. But there are other symptoms to explain a diagnosis of schizophrenia, and some of these are:

False beliefs that are not based on reality.

Hallucinations which are hearing or seeing things which don't exist.

Disorganised thinking which is diagnosed through disorganised speech.

Extremely disorganised or abnormal motor behaviour.

Depression and social withdrawal

Hostility, suspiciousness, and extreme reaction to criticism

These are worrying symptoms for anyone, and even though they may not suggest schizophrenia, they should never be ignored, and professional help should be sought.

This book is focused on the everyday internal 'voices' that most people report experiencing.

For some, they are just thoughts that suggest actions that may or may not be helpful.

For some, the thoughts may be more urgent in speaking about more painful memories and events in our lives.

For some, the thoughts are definitely perceived as voices and may sound like our own voices or as if the voice is speaking directly to us, but this voice is still contained in our minds and is not perceived as externally audible.

As I have begun to explain the act of 'talking' to ourselves, I have found it easier to think of this process as 'thought talk,' and I believe they are both subtly different but also seemingly the same. Here are some examples of thought talk.

"I better get up now; I've got a lot to do. It's late really; I should have got up earlier, I'm an idiot, and now I've ruined my whole day by being lazy."

Most people have a running commentary in their head, something similar to this; it is usually like a voice-over in a documentary. It speaks aggressively sometimes and could be described as a bully. I once had a client who really believed that if she didn't listen to this voice, then she would never get anything done. I could see the way that this worked in her favour, and even though I usually steer my clients towards a gentler sounding voice, in this case, it seemed better not to disturb this belief in her as this voice was being very protective in getting her to show up in her life and get things done. This type of voice can speak in the first person, but is also capable of chatting to you as another voice, that does not sound like 'you'.

"Oh, it's ok to be a bit late getting up; I've got loads of time. I'll just start my day again from now. It will get better. I'm ok now. I feel more balanced. I'm good."

This is a more friendly-sounding voice, and we may experience an inner voice like this when we are in a good mood or when our life is or seems easier to deal with. I have wondered whether stress of some kind causes our voices to become more insistent, more nasty, and bullying. I think that this is mostly true, but I also know that some people are plagued by a much nastier version more than others, even though most people can experience both kinds of voices.

"You're doing ok. Why worry so much? It will be ok. Things usually work out for you, don't they? You're a good guy at the heart of you. I like you."

This affable voice can also speak in the third person and sounds as if he really likes you. I don't believe that this is anywhere near the norm for most people, mostly because it is the category of an unconscious running commentary, and on this level, we hardly even register it as a voice or even a thought. It may feel comforting and safe, and because we enjoy its manner, it slips into our consciousness as a soothing mechanism. Some of you may only just realise from reading this that you do have such an inner voice, which could be a pleasant surprise and something to build on.

"I am so ashamed of myself. I hate myself. I'm a really bad person, and no one likes me.'

This thought voice is talking in the first person, talking as if it is us and talking in a really nasty way, but also slightly pitying itself, as if it is stuck in a trap and has no way out; it sounds hopeless. When our inner voice talks about hating us, it is usually very hurtful and upsetting to us, and this is entirely understandable; who wants to be spoken to like this? No one would enjoy it, and yet it is what millions of people do every day of their lives. I think that this is one of the most common internal voice types and that this is a very sad voice.

"There's no fucking point, none at all. You might as well just give up. No one gives a crap about what you're doing, about your shitty little life. No one has ever cared about you, and no one really likes you anyway. Just fucking stop pretending. You are a complete dick head; you may as well just fuck off and die. I hate you!"

This example has a similar kind of anger and hatred, but there is none of the self-pity because it is talking in the third person and has no concept of being 'you.' This seems different and probably the most severe and nastier thought voice, the voice that is not you and that hates you. I think that this is the darkest voice of a deeply embedded self-hatred that can lead to suicidal thoughts, which are sometimes acted out.

This is a voice that is not on your side and appears to hate you. Once we become aware of this kind of voice, we can more clearly see the internal division in our psyche. We now have an internal voice that actively hates us and appears to be standing some distance away from us, and seems to be an authority on our behaviour. If you discover that this is the main way that your internal voice speaks to you, it could be time to seek therapeutic help. A therapist can guide and support you through the more difficult path of discovering that there is a voice that sounds like someone else living in your head that hates you. A therapist won't think you are ill of you or judge you for having these thoughts or voices. But rather, they will understand and support you to do the inner work needed.

If this book can, at the very least, help you to see the destructive voices that can harm your sense of self and the choices you could make, perhaps never living up to your potential. Then I think that I have done a good job, and there may be a lot more that you can get out of it to help you feel better about yourself.   But as this is a self-help book, and as such, there should be a warning that could be applied to any self-help book. Please read the book, absorb the concepts, and try some of the changes to see if they can work for you. But be aware that if you are feeling alone, if you don't have a close family or a support group, then you may need to seek out help and support as a first step.

These voices can go on for years, and it seems to me that most people just absorb them into their personality under the shorthand heading of "that's just part of me." Or we may think of it as a hidden part of us, and we don't really want to expose the secret thoughts we have, and we definitely don't want to speak of the nasty and exposing voices that scream their hatred at us.

So as with most hidden things, we get mired in shame which then eats at our core sense of self, especially if there is a long and intensive history with shame.

Four

Shame

They cry in the dark, so you can't see

their tears

They hide in the light, so you can't see their

fears

Forgive and forget, all the while

Love and pain become one and the same

In the eyes of the wounded child

Because hell is for children

Song: Hell is for children

Album: Crimes of passion

Artist: Pat Benatar 1980

Shame is one of the cornerstones of a dysfunctional family, unhappiness, and co-dependency. It is the backbone of all addictions, and it is always toxic in nature. Brene Brown is famous for her first Ted talk on YouTube, which was about the nature of shame and her own journey through it; she concluded that shame serves no purpose but is simply a source of suffering.

Shame is not the same as guilt or the same as 'feeling ashamed,' which is when we have done something wrong as an adult with responsibility and for which we are ashamed and will most likely feel guilty about what we have done.

Shame is a deeply held sense of being wrong that is linked to feelings of unworthiness and low self-esteem, and sufferers of shame are often scared that if they told someone about this shame, not only might they risk feeling judged, but they may find out that it really was all their fault because they already feel so internally 'bad.'

Toxic shame leads to chronic negative emotions or behaviours that harm self or others, and people with this chronic shame may believe that they are unworthy of love. They may feel afraid of connecting to others in case they are seen as the bad person they believe that they are, and they would then be rejected.

These are some of the difficulties that chronic shame can cause:

- Trouble forming and sustaining romantic relationships or friendships.

- Feelings of isolation and loneliness.

- Difficulty being honest in interpersonal relationships.

- Seems like a matter of life and death to keep the internal self-hidden.

- Getting into abusive relationships.

- Substance abuse.

- Compulsive behaviours such as shopping or gambling.

- Workaholism

Shame is linked to addictive and compulsive behaviours and has also been linked in studies to suicidal thoughts and actions. In fact, most of these fears are so closely linked to low self-esteem that it is impossible to divide the two aspects. People with low self-esteem would have all of the above difficulties in the same areas, so would it be true that all people with low self-esteem suffer from shame? I do think that this is true, and it is this aspect of internal 'wrongness' and 'badness' that makes it very difficult to heal low self-esteem.

I can remember that when I fully realised that I had extremely low self-esteem, it seemed impossible to feel better about myself, whatever I said, did, or achieved. I then began to understand that it was the presence of shame that made it so much more difficult, as I truly believed that I was useless and bad to the core and could not change. Therefore, if my belief in my own badness was so complete, how can I possibly do things differently or change this faulty perspective? I remember thinking as if shame did not live in my head but rather ran through my veins and was so entwined with my sense of self that I could never separate myself from it.

Shame can be problematic when it becomes internalised and results in an overly harsh evaluation of oneself as a whole person. This inner critic might tell you that you are a bad person, worthless, or have no value. The truth is, how deeply you feel ashamed often has little to do with your worth or what you have done wrong. Shame is pervasive and is difficult to identify in oneself. But the clues that you are suffering because of shame could be low self-esteem, a sense of not being 'good enough,' a belief that you are a bad person. Shame is visible in the internal voices, and this is one of the ways that it conveys our feelings of uselessness to ourselves. It is a self-perpetuating system, and it can continue forever if it isn't discovered. I have met many older people as clients or colleagues, and friends who show these behaviours externally but have never even thought to do something different or to seek help. Shame and our internal voices are, by their very nature, secretive and of course, shameful. So help is never sought or asked for, and sadly, many people suffer in silence.

Shame could actually be considered a 'hidden' illness because it is pervasive, intrusive, damaging, life threatening and most of all secretive.

Five

Co-Dependency

People are strange....when you're a stranger

Faces look ugly....when you're alone

Women seem wicked....when you're unwanted

Streets are uneven...when you're down

When you're strange.....faces come out of the rain

When your strange....no one remembers your name

When your strange

People are strange...when your a stranger

Song: People are strange

Artist: The Doors

Album: Strange Days 1967

Co-dependency is a theory that tries to explain the imbalance in relationships where one person enables another person's self-destructive behaviour, such as addictions, poor mental health, immaturity, irresponsibility, or underachievement. Co-dependency is the house that shame lives in. Co-dependency is a disease that deteriorates the soul and affects the sufferers' personal life, families, relatives, businesses and careers, health, and spiritual growth. Co-dependency is debilitating and, if left untreated, causes us to become more destructive to ourselves and to others.

The definitions of co-dependency vary but typically include self-sacrifice, a focus on others' needs, and attempts to fix other people's problems for them. It is usually more invasive towards romantic partners and one's own children but also can be seen in friendships, family members, or co-workers. People can also be unhealthily attached to inanimate objects too, and in fact, I see this as an attachment that causes a person to attempt to get his needs met by fixating on someone or something else. Co-dependency is a form of self-abandonment and I could also think of alcohol or drugs as a codependent 'object' used to abandon self, growth and life.

The term Co-dependency has been most often associated with Alcoholics Anonymous with the realisation that Alcoholism is not solely about the addict. It is also about the family and friends who make up a network for the Alcoholic, that may appear concerned and caring. But can, in fact, be overly concerned, self-seeking and destructive to the process of an addict getting well and facing what he needs to face up to in order to break his denial.

The dysfunction of the alcoholic family can appear to be caused by the "addicted' person, but in fact, it is the co-partner who is also in denial, obsessed with fixing, and sometimes just as crazy in their behaviours as the addict is in using substances.

There have been numerous books written, and theories widened over the years. In 1983 Janet G Woititz brought out the book *Adult Children of Alcoholics,* sold 2 million copies, and was on the New York best-seller list for almost a year.

Family therapist Robin Norwood's book *Women who love too much* came out in 1985, and it aimed to help women who were addicted to men who offered little love in return. This book sold over two million copies in its first year and is still selling and remains relative now. It has been published in many languages and is selling well on audio even today.

In 1986 Melody Beaty popularised the concept further with her book *Co-dependency No More* sold eight million copies, and as before, this book is still selling well and is also in audio and printed in many languages. She drew on her personal experiences and those of caring for someone with addictions. Her work underpinned the twelve-step fellowship of Codependents Anonymous, founded in 1986, and the group has by themselves developed further understanding of the condition.

Definition

Co-Dependency has no established or diagnostic criteria within the mental health community, and it has never been included as a condition in any edition of the DSM. But Tim Cormak, a psychiatrist who tried without success to get it included, wrote, "Co-dependency is a recognisable pattern of personality traits, predictably found with most members of substance misuse families, which are capable of creating sufficient dysfunction to warrant inclusion in the DSM 111

Some of the characteristics of co-dependency are listed in the Co-dependents Anonymous book (1995) as:

Denial Patterns

Difficulty identifying feelings, minimising, altering, or denying feelings.

Perceiving themselves as being completely unselfish and dedicated to the well-being of others.

Low Self- Esteem Patterns

Difficulty making decisions.

Judging their thoughts, words and actions as never being good enough.

Embarrassed to receive recognition, praise of gifts.

Unable to ask others to meet their needs or wants.

Value other people's approval of their thoughts, feelings, and behaviour over self-approval.

Compliance Patterns

Compromise their values and integrity to avoid rejection and other people's anger.

Sensitive to others' feelings and assumes the same feelings.

Extremely loyal, remaining in harmful situations too long.

Places a higher value on others' opinions and feelings and are too afraid to express differing

viewpoints or feelings.

Puts aside personal interests and hobbies to do what others want.

Accepts sex as a substitute for love.

Control Patterns

Believes that most others are incapable of taking care of themselves.

Attempts to convince others what they should think and feel.

Come resentful when others refuse their offers of help.

Freely offer advice and guidance without being asked.

Lavish gifts and favours on those they care about.

Uses sex to gain approval and acceptance.

The book of Co-dependants Anonymous is full of stories of people who identify as having these patterns and speaking about how their lives have been affected by most, if not all of them. It is a great book to understand many of the patterns of behaviour of people who grow up in dysfunctional families, whatever the behaviours displayed.

Family Dynamics

Don't make the mistake of thinking that codependency is only formed in alcoholic or addicted families because even though this is where it was first observed, through the families of alcoholics. The category has more recently been widened to include adult children from ANY family with dysfunction as its main characteristic, because dysfunctional families are where the inner child emerges, covered in shame.

Within the dysfunctional family, it is the child who learns to become attuned to the parent's needs and feelings instead of the other way around. Parenting requires a certain level of self-sacrifice and giving a Child's needs a high priority.

Generally, a parent who takes care of their own needs (emotional & Physical) in a healthy way will be a better caregiver, whereas co-dependent parents may be less effective or even do harm to a child. The needs of a co-dependant are constant, and a child within this system cannot fail to suffer from these consequences.

Children of these parents who are ignored and their feelings negated will consequently ignore and negate their own feelings and are very likely to become co-dependants themselves as adults who ignore their own feelings and have many unmet needs.

Six

SUB PERSONALTIES and SPLITTING

"Thus the individual is not a single self, but many selves,

which change somewhat as the individual shifts from situation to situation

and person to person.

We are, in short, what the situation demands.

Patrica Niles Middlebrook (1936-2019)

It seemed very important to include in this book some amount of theoretical information on the subject of the splitting of the self. This is especially true for me because I was trained in a psychological discipline that consisted of the idea of internal splitting at the centre of its theory base, this is Transactional Analysis, its founder was Eric Berne. The name of this theory can sound very complicated, but in fact, uses everyday language in its theory and application, because he especially wanted it to be accessible to ordinary people and to make it much easier to understand.

Eric Berne was one of the many people putting forward this theory of 'splitting' that was becoming popular in the 20th century. 'Splitting' being the way in which the human psyche splits itself into different and somewhat separate parts of the personality.

The theory probably started with **Sigmund Freud,** who was credited as the father of psychoanalysis in the early part of the 20th century, and his most important theory of the **ego, the id, and the superego, w**hich is the first theory that breaks the self into separate parts.

Carl Jung then talked in his language about the **complexes** or **archetypes.**

Paul Federn, Eric Berne, and John Watkins all used the idea of Ego States.

Kurt Lewin used the language of calling them **sub regions of the personality.**

Fritz Perls used the vernacular, top **dog-underdog.**

Klein, Fairburn & Gungrip all talked separately about the theory of internal objects.

Balint talked about the **child in the patient.**

Hilgard talked about the **internal observer.**

Stone & Wilkemen used the description of **energy patterns**

Mair talked about a **community of self.**

Assagioli & Redfern used the description **sub personalities**

Personally, I have liked the fuller definition given by **John Rowan,** whose book helped me to clarify my thinking about these separate identities.

(Subpersonalities 1990) When he used the sentence:

"A sub-personality is a semi-permanent and semi-autonomous region of the personality capable of acting as a person.

It concerns me that some people say that they don't believe in the inner child concept. The theory is solidly based on this process of splitting; we split off parts of our personality that we cannot understand or handle emotionally. As children, we cannot handle any strong adult emotions because we don't have the understanding or the experience to be able to process them. Children are just not emotionally equipped for when a parent is very angry or punishing; the child has a strong desire to get away from the adult and, in their fear and their desire to run away, may split off parts of themselves or even take in and split the angry part of the adult internally. This is the process of the birth of an inner child part of the self and is more widely accepted these days, to the extent that now almost everyone has heard of some of the phrases or words, such as "my inner child" or "my internal worrier" and "I feel sad, and I think it's my child self."

We are used to this perspective, and we understand it because it fits with our experiences. This is important because then we can measure what we experience with what theory says and this is the best use of theory when we use it to prove or disprove what our own experience tells us.

When a child experiences anger, judgement, or bullying from a parent, the only way to deal with this is to split it off from his idea of self in order to preserve some sense of being ok. Children cannot bear the idea that their parents are behaving in this way towards them. It is easier for children to believe that they are bad or wrong and the 'bad' part of the parent or persecutor is literally 'taken in,' meaning that the angry, scary voice is absorbed into the child's psyche but surrounded by the protection of 'this is not me,' it is then split off from the child's conscious awareness and remains internalised and walled off.

So when this voice speaks to the adult in 'thought talk,' the angry voice is the same as the internalised parental voice. Whether it is speaking angrily to others or talking to the adult directly, it is in this angry parental voice. This voice may seem separate; they may think of it as 'not me,' and it is sometimes called an introject. Whatever we call it, and however we experience it, it is usually a powerful voice because of its parental status from whom it came, and the person experiencing this will often find it very difficult to think clearly or to act autonomously when this 'parent' is calling the shots.

Freud's original understanding of splitting and his divisions of the id, ego, and superego have changed over the past hundred years, and these 'splits' have been changed and adapted over time by different theorists. What has not changed though, is that people will split off parts of themselves under extreme stress and/or pressure, trauma or fear.

Defence Mechanisms

The theory of defence mechanisms describes the way that adults deny their reality in order to avoid unpleasant events, feelings, or thoughts. Most defences come from the unconscious part of our mind in the desire to escape life, consequences, reality, or any difficult situation that an adult does not want to face. Though we may be unaware of our behaviour, it often appears odd to others.

- **Denial** is one of the most common defence mechanisms. It is used to refuse to accept the reality which then avoids difficult thoughts or feelings and can be completely blocked from the rational mind.

- **Repression** is where difficult thoughts or painful memories can be upsetting and then can unconsciously be hidden. But the memory cannot fully be forgotten and can continue to interfere with behaviour from an unconscious place.

- **Projection** is when we may have thoughts or feelings about ourselves or others that we find uncomfortable. So we may 'project' those attributes onto another person and disown them in ourselves.

- **Displacement** is when you direct strong emotions and frustrations toward another person or object that doesn't feel threatening. This then allows you to satisfy an impulse to react, but at no risk to yourself.

- **Regression** is when some people who feel threatened or anxious may regress to an earlier stage of development, seeking safety. Examples include bedwetting in children who are worried. Chain smoking and overeating can be an example of anxiety in adults.

- **Rationalisation** is when people try to explain undesirable behaviour, which may make them feel better about the event or circumstance.

- **Sublimation** is often seen as a healthy defence mechanism. Choosing to direct strong emotion into a safe object or environment, like boxing or running.

- **Reaction formation** is when people know what they are feeling but choose to present another feeling that is more positive and, therefore, not real but feels safer to express.

- **Compartmentalisation** has people separating areas of their lives so as to protect themselves and keep life simpler.

- **Intellectualisation** is choosing to remove all emotion from a difficult situation by removing

- emotional responses and just staying with the facts.

These methods of avoiding difficult feelings, actions, or relationship responsibilities are supposed to make life easier, but in reality, it never works that way. The person using these unconscious tools will usually make his life and relationships more complicated.

Once again, when we use these shortcut defences, it can be helpful for us to become aware of what we are doing in order to notice and make changes over time. I once had a trainer who would always insist that we clean up our language, and her favourite saying was, "Say it straight, or it will come out crooked."

This is good advice to practice when we want to get clearer with our communications and at the same time practice clarity in our relationships, which in turn leads to simpler and more honest dialogue with others

Seven

The Inner Child

When the rain is blowing in your face.

And the whole world is on your case

I could offer you a warm embrace.

To make you feel my love

When the evening shadows and the stars
appear

And then there is no one out there to dry your
tears

I could hold you for a million year

To make you feel feel my love

Artist: Bob Dylan

Album: Time out of mind

Song: To make you feel my. Love.

Growing

The inner child is not simply our actual child as she was in the past, or our adult just 'remembering' things about the past. The inner child is not the one born at the physical birth.

The inner child is made from a reaction to a feeling of fear, pain, shock, or horror at something that happened in the reality of the past.

The trauma is then frozen in time, and with this freezing, one of the Child's defences is to split off a part of themselves. Then the memory or indeed any aspect that can't be integrated into the child's understanding of his life is 'split' away from the main personality and becomes 'stunted' in its growth pattern, thus remaining a traumatised 'child' forever.

Because try as they might, children do not have the tools or the understanding to handle the complex feelings being generated internally. The inner child is born at these times of trauma and great stress.

This 'split off' part of him then becomes a 'stuck' part of the child, who is completely walled off in the psyche and, instead of growing up chronologically, remains forever in the trauma, reliving the events and is forever 'the damaged child.'

Also, this event can become even more complex when different traumas happen at different times in childhood. The one that happened when the child was only four is already born and holding its own beliefs about the world and others so that when another painful event occurs, say, a few years later, it is not absorbed into this existing inner child. It becomes a new 'inner child' born from the experiences of a different kind, occurring at a different age and becoming a different split-off part at a new age, having his own childlike understanding about life and others in the world.

Whether he is safe or not, whether he can rely on his parents, whether they love him enough to care about him? Children are vulnerable creatures who are brand new to this world, they are sensitive and attuned to the emotions of their caregivers, and their very life depends on this attunement. It is the reason why babies have such big eyes. Babies' eyes are adult-size because it is their only device to survive bonding with their parents by being appealing and lovable. It doesn't always work out that way, of course, and babies can experience rejection at birth in so many ways, adoption, the mother's inability to bond for many reasons, post-natal depression, the child's ill health, parental illness or death, and all of these events can have an impact on the attachment process.

But because babies are so sweetly vulnerable, this defence mostly works well for them until they are older, but between 2 and 4 years, the ego develops in the child, and this is the time of separation. A difficult time for parents and the child. So many potentially harmful events can hurt a small child's sense of dignity and importance in the world. Then it becomes time to attend school, and other important figures are also able to impact the child's understanding of relationships, the world, and where he fits in. These days peer pressure can be so destructive in children from around the age of 7 or 8, and the struggle for survival can seem very real and threatening when faced with bullying, peer pressure, child poverty, lack, and social media. This is why it is so important for children to not only feel safe and loved but to feel accepted and valued so that they have a robust inner world and the ability to be self-soothing.

The next struggle is around 11-15 years when the child is becoming a teenager, and at this time, not only do they experience all of the same problems that a seven-year-old was facing, but the difficulties posed are heightened because of the introduction of massive hormonal changes, physically, emotionally and mentally. He becomes angry, argumentative, aggressive, and fearful, and can experience violent changes in moods and needs. One moment demanding everything from his parents; the next wanting to be hugged and reassured. Parents may also suffer from the lack of good enough parenting that they have received in their childhood and can often worry about what they are passing on to their children.

Childhood is a difficult time for everyone involved and for those who go through it, wait a minute, that's everyone! We all have to manoeuvre these difficult transitions and somehow survive. Even people who describe idyllic childhoods will have experienced some kind of disappointment, emotional difficulty, problems at school, the teenage years, loss, and sadness. No one escapes childhood; we learn from it, we grow from it, and we become the person who carries their own particular brand of baggage.

Seeking help.

We now understand a bit more how the inner child is made and how she is affected by the events she has suffered but survived in her childhood. People come to therapy or read these kinds of self-help books, mostly because their past is impacting on their present, and they want to heal their present.

Most don't even know that there is a link between what happened and what is happening now. When I talk to people about their painful memories of the past, most people don't want to talk about those events even though the pain can be seen in their eyes, and there are many reasons why people don't want these difficult conversations:

 "I don't want to speak bad of my parents."

"It's too painful to remember."

"I think I was a bad child, and my parents found me difficult"

"What's the point of dragging all those memories up."

"But it all happened so long ago, and there's nothing that can be done now."

"It wasn't that bad though."

These are the walking wounded and they often have careers and partners; they may have children and a life that is often happy. But internally, there is a disconnect, and adults wear many masks to hide their wounded sense of themselves. There is no space for thinking that this internal world could feel any better, and they are often under the belief that life is often difficult, but they put on a brave front, "it must be like this for everyone." This may be conveyed in a victim manner, poor me, or they may just shrug and accept their fate.

These are the vast majority of people just going through the motions because when the inner child does not have a part in adult life, so much more than bad memories are lost. This inner child part of us also carries joy, wisdom, and creativity, and the adult isn't even aware that this is a missing part of them; they can laugh and enjoy the peak moments, but sometimes even these moments are hollow, and it feels like, just going through the motions.

Then they will shrug and turn away or have a drink to push the uneasy feeling away, they might say that their life is mostly OK. But the inner child is alive and living alone deep in the basement of the psyche, emitting its feelings of loneliness like a lighthouse beacon and hoping that someone will see the signal and respond.

Some people, though, have very clear memories, and they accept that those memories are not good. Sometimes they remember that really bad things happened to them in their childhood. They may have been just about clinging on for years, self-medicating, self-harming, maybe in poor relationships. These people are the wounded but not walking so well; they often have disruptive and difficult relationships, and then find themselves frequently alone and sad. They can suffer from an attachment disorder and may have had a diagnosis of borderline personality, or PTSD and be known to psychiatric services. These people are very hurt and barely clinging on to life and certainly not having much joy. I believe this book can also help these people to understand their process better and to see more clearly how the inner child is undermining their ability to function as they would like to.

These people may need the help of a therapist or counsellor to support them in facing the more difficult challenges from their childhood. Their inner child is still in the basement but is much more vocal and disruptive. She is often very angry; she can be destructive and is not content to sit alone and deal with the feelings herself. She wants help and attention, and she wants it now.

I believe that, like many other processes, the events of our childhood are on a continuum, which starts from one end and goes through many stages to the other end. There is a lot of information and tests online these days to consider what is now called Adverse Childhood Experiences (ACES), and society is becoming much better at understanding these effects on children and how damaging they can be in many areas of adult life.

What society is less good at is recognising the ways that adults with a damaged inner child might behave or need help.

Extreme Abuse-Violence-Neglect-Trauma-Loss-Cruelty-Rejection-Anger-Emotional damage

This is a very sad line, wherever you look at it, and if you have suffered from any of these events, then you will have an inner child who is either sad or extremely sad and angry. We also know that the frequency of events is significant too. If Parents lose their temper on very few and rare occasions, the child may be able to cope with this. We know that what can change a traumatic event for anybody is having someone to comfort us, someone who is kind, compassionate, and willing to put their own needs to one side to help us to regulate our emotions; this is especially true for children. Sometimes the occasional presence of a caring grandparent can have the most profound effect on the child's experiences. The child's feelings will not be negated, but the child will be immensely helped by having someone to give some love and care, thus helping the child to make better beliefs about the world around them and themselves.

Clarity

Here are statements that make it even clearer what the inner child is:

1.   The inner child is a real and felt experience that works like this; When we were children, we were taught how to behave, what to believe, how to think, how to feel, and how to express ourselves by our caregivers. Parents, teachers, babysitters, etc., anyone who had some higher control or influence over us had power over us.

2.   These parents or parent figures also had messages of the same kind, passed onto them from their parents or teachers. Most of these messages are authoritarian, judgemental, and controlling and come from an earlier generation that did not understand either child development or psychology. So the messages received by most children since victorian times have been of the harsher kind.

3.   Even today, parents who know and understand better are still infected by the messages of previous generations because of the way that these messages are passed down. They travel on and exist in the minds of children because that is the most fertile

ground, and children are the most vulnerable people in the world.

4. It is us, as actual children, who hear these careless, judgemental, and damaging words that have been passed on for many years. It is important to understand how the child interprets the meaning of the message and how he uses it in his own future.

5. The child hears "you are stupid," and the words seem very real. More so if they are backed up by actions, such as shouting, a belittling voice, and often physical attack. If this is said frequently enough, it becomes more believable and real to the child and is stored this away in the psyche to be made into a solid belief of "I am stupid."

6. Another deeper aspect of this sad story is that a child cannot hold the fact that their parents may be bad. So he has to make himself bad, and because he does not understand why he is bad or why his parents don't "act' as if they like him, he must split this knowledge from his sense of self in order to survive the pain of having parents who may not seem to like or love him. Therefore hiding a part of himself in a secret belief that seems absolutely true.

7. This process can be repeated many times and with even stronger feelings from the parent (or caregiver), especially if the adult in charge has his own unhealed trauma

from his early childhood. In the form of physical abuse, emotional neglect, sexual abuse, and with the added components of regularity and severity, harshness and violence.

8. Every child has to find a way to survive even the smallest acts of emotional neglect in order to feel that everything is OK and that they are actually cared for by loving parents. It is easier for a child to be angry at himself than at his parents because it is unthinkable to a child that he is not loved and cared for by his parents. So the split is complete, and the child has a part or parts of himself that he dislikes or hates inside himself now.

9. When we are grown up and become real adults, we carry these beliefs about life in many ways and are often in denial of the events from our childhood.

• Sometimes adults believe that they had an ideal childhood….denial.

• Sometimes not being able to remember much about their childhood…denial, and repression.

• Sometimes adults cannot bear to re-experience childhood pain, especially extreme forms of traumatic and dramatic occurrences….disassociation.

• Sometimes as unhappiness… self-blaming.

- Sometimes as struggling in relationships... self-blaming or blaming the other.

- Sometimes having a lack of self-care... self-harming.

- Sometimes using alcohol or drugs...self-harming, self-hatred, and denial.

- Sometimes self-harming and suicidal thoughts.... Depression, giving up, self-hatred. Some children grow up knowing that a lot of their problems are due to the way they were treated in their family, and they may be blamed or angry or even remain frightened of their parents and break the relationship with them.

10. This rescuer must be you. You must be the saviour that your own inner child needs. I ask my clients to imagine a child that they know, seeing it suffering and in deep sadness and loneliness; what would they do? Most answer that they would rush to its aid. But then they are not so quick to get to their own suffering child, and it's the same for everyone.

11. Once they know about it, people want to get as far away from this inner child as possible; they have had years of torment from the child, who has been projecting its misery and anger onto the adult you. The adult (YOU) is covering his ears and cannot stand to hear it anymore.

12. We try to find a way of getting rid of it and have been doing this for most of our lives. Not listening, not understanding, not helping, not seeing. In fact we are perpetuating our own misery.

13. It is now time to stop doing this and face some aspects of your life and yourself that would be helpful to look at in order to feel better and accept yourself for who you are and for what you have experienced. To become a whole person, with integrated memories and beliefs that are your own.

This is a comprehensive but not exhaustive list of the ways that a traumatised child is made and then grows into an adult.

I discuss the steps to take, in order, to begin a healing process in Chapter 10. This is where you will find a direct way to make the changes that will help you to be happier and to have a healthier relationship with your inner child and, therefore, with yourself.

You may decide not to do it, and of course, that is your choice, but there was a reason you chose this book, and it would be a real shame for you not to follow it through. Yes, it may seem difficult, and to some, it may feel impossible, but I promise you it is not impossible, but it may be difficult sometimes.

If you feel really overwhelmed and cannot even bear the thought of proceeding, I suggest again, that you might need the support of a therapist to walk you through the process. It could be a TA therapist or a counsellor or therapist who advertises that they work with the inner child. This will apply to adults who know that they were neglected or abused physically, emotionally, or sexually by their parents, caregivers, or any adult who told them things or had expectations of them that should not have occurred. Even if you only suspect you were damaged by childhood adversity, you may not be fully remembering what happened and may also need to speak to a professional to discover hidden or lost.

Eight

Client's Process.

Oh the sisters of mercy, they are not departed
or gone

They are waiting for me, when I thought that I
just can't go on

And they brought me their comfort and later
they brought me this song

Oh I hope you run into them, You, who've been
travelling so long

Yes you who must leave everything that you
cannot control

It begins with your family

But soon it comes round to your soul.

Well, I've been where your hanging and I think,

I can see how you're pinned

When your not feeling holy. Your loneliness says
that you've sinned.

Song: Sisters of Mercy

Album: Songs of Leonard Cohen 1967

Artist: Leonard Cohen

I feel as if my training to become a psychotherapist over 18 years ago has been such a gift in my life. Because in the search for my own healing, I have been given the tools to help others to discover their own needs and their own painful thoughts, interactions, and belief systems.

I hope that by describing some of my client's processes and presenting problems, you will gain some further insight and identification with this problem of 'what to do with the inner child'!   I want to give you some more examples so that you can see the similarities that could help you to understand your own actions and thought talk.

None of these stories are based on one particular client because I am mindful of anonymity, and also I have worked with many clients with similar problems. So this chapter is the result of mixing up their identities up but still using the essence of the ways that people can become stuck and the means by which release is found.

I believe that stories, as well as metaphor, simile, and understanding, are the means by which we begin to discover more about ourselves. For me, the first discoveries came from reading self-help books and finding myself in the stories about real people struggling with real problems that I also seemed to be enmeshed with.

As humans, identification with others people helps us to feel connected, takes away our sense of loneliness, and provides us with some hope. We know that someone else has taken action to change these feelings. Even if we cannot imagine making those changes, we can dream about the possibility of change, and we can allow ourselves to acknowledge the desire for something to be different.

Not all of my clients have needed to find inner child healing or have worked on clearing up their self-talk. But a great many of them have walked this particular path of healing those aspects of themselves that have been stuck for many years.

Every client eventually asks me the same question, and I always have the same answer.

The question will come at some time in the therapy when my client has explained to me what they think their problem is. Their 'problem' is usually explained as if there is something wrong with them. Personally, I have a bad temper, and I drink too much. I want my sparkle back or any number of similar thoughts. The upshot seems to be that there is something wrong with them, and they want to know how to change this perceived 'bad' habit that they appear to have.

I will usually outline the problem back to them to be sure I have understood some of the story as told from their perspective, and then tell them what

I see the problem to be. Clients are often shocked by this; if they haven't done any counselling or therapy before, they may have a vague idea that I am someone who will just listen to them and their story without any intervention. But the way that I approach therapy is with compassion and honesty, and I find it easy to say exactly what I see and understand from the clients words and actions. I notice body gestures and the clues there; I notice particular words that are used frequently. I listen to how they tell their story, the intonation, and the gaps they leave. I use my intuition to 'feel' into their emotional and internal pain to see if these things are congruent for them. I receive a lot of feedback from these observations, and it is then easier to make suggestions of what the client may need to do next.

I then give a client the news that is not always taken too well:

 "your problem looks to me as if it is coming from the past."

"From the past?, but It's about what's happening now, it's about my partner, or it's about my anger; how is it about the past?"

So I explain a lot of what I have said here in this book, that if we encountered trauma in our younger life, we will feel it now because trauma limits us and stops us from becoming who we could become. It limits us mostly by recurring fear about our decisions, finances, and security. In fact, almost anything can become 'fear food' for the mind.

That this trauma stays stuck in the body and in the memories.

That you have an inner child part who is stuck in some trauma drama and is living, as if it is still the past, in fear and sadness.

That you are not one unified self, but there are many differing aspects that cause you to feel crazy sometimes and to ask, "How can I think one thing so strongly and yet do another thing entirely?"

That it is up to you to make contact with this part of you, to recognise its fears, to take care of it, and this means really facing up to being an adult with responsibilities to yourself.

This is the point where clients often say:

"So how do I do that? I don't understand it; I don't even know where to start!"

Maybe you have had the same thoughts as you work through this book?

So then I tell them the good news, and here it is:

"It is a wonderful thing to begin a journey of knowing who you are, most people want to know the answer to this question, and it's a legitimate question. But if you leave out your trauma and ignore the hurt that you went through, then you cannot fully know yourself, and large parts of you are missing.

You have started this journey already by coming to therapy or choosing a book about the inner child, some method of knowing what needs to happen in order for your life to be easier to manage because there is an awareness that something isn't right and needs to change."

Most people are relieved when I tell them that I know how to heal this 'child' from the past, and that I can help and support them, and so the journey begins.

I think of this therapy with my clients as 'having heroic conversations' . I believe that all 'broken' people are indeed heroes and have often been struggling for the biggest part of their lives, with their own, often very heavy burdens. (Solution Focused Approach. Elliot Connie)

Does evil exist?

This client was very keen to do this work even though she had previously experienced quite a few years of therapy, discovering many things about herself that had helped her to grow and mature. She was extremely clever, and she knew all of the theories that I have talked about here, and she knew them much better than I did.

But she came for some more therapy because she wanted to be able to tell someone that she thought that her mother was evil and it seemed as if this was one of her most deeply held fears. The fear of 'what if' it was true and evil existed in the world.

It was the first time that she had been able to utter these fears into words. The relief from being heard in a safe space brought a great deal of relief that was clearly visible on her face. She had allowed herself to admit her deeply hidden and disturbing thoughts.

The really important part of this vulnerability was the fear of being judged or diagnosed, nor did she want her experience minimised by anyone. This fear may have lived mostly in her child but as I have attempted to explain previously, the beliefs of the child literally become the fears and beliefs of the adult self. Wherever the beliefs were held, she wanted this truth about her experience to be deeply heard and believed by another person.

She had found a safe place where she was able to explore her experiences of living with a mother who had severe mental health problems, at the very least. Was her mother evil? We discussed this a lot and never really came to a firm conclusion. I suggested that she read a book with the title, The People of the Lie, written by M Scott peck, he is a priest, a writer, and a therapist, and he strongly believes that evil does exist. It's a very interesting theory that rings very true in certain cases cases.

The primary work that we did together was to get in touch with the deeply traumatised child, who was terrified of the evil that she saw daily, in her mother's eyes and actions. This part of her was too scared to speak out for such a long time, and my client was actively involved in doing her best to keep this inner child hidden. Even though she really wanted to help herself to change, for a long time, she could only continue to do that which she had done all her life, which was to hide her pain.

It is the hiding of the pain that turns it into shame, the child becomes ashamed of the parents actions, as if they themselves were somehow responsible for what was done to them. The process for the 'damaged child' is something along these lines, if my mother doesn't love me, then I must be unlovable and as I don't know how to make myself lovable, I must be very bad indeed. This is the exact process of how shame is involved all the way through, the experiencing of the wrongness of the self, the internalisation of shame and the making of negative beliefs about ones self, then the pushing away and the compulsive hiding of our own damaged self.

It is for this reason that very traumatised people may need the help a therapist to say the right words, and to hold a safe space, where it is even safe to tell the deepest hidden truths. Very slowly, over time, this client began talking about how it was to be terrorised, to be played mind games with, to be denied food, water, and love. This torture was acted out by a mother's cruel behaviour, and my client has grappled for years with the question "was her mother mentally ill or was she cruel and/or possessed by some kind of evil.

This client remembered these details cognitively; she knew what had happened to her all too well. But it took a long time for her to be able to allow the feelings of terror from the child to enter into her psyche because to feel that amount of fear as a child was an immense task that is often far too big and heavy for even the adult self to carry. The only safety that this young girl had, was to split off in order to be able to hold all of those frightening feelings. She had held them hidden for most of her life, up to this point, where she was allowed to speak and eventually to begin to release the fears of her, sad, and lonely self.

To be known and seen at this deepest level is usually a great relief to most clients, but it is also a very painful relief, and one of the most important and difficult emotional questions, for the adult and the inner child is "who am I if my parents didn't love me?"

This wonderfully brave client would tell you herself that she has accepted what happened to her in her past. It wasn't right at all; it was terrifying for her, but she survived, and now I believe that she would refer to herself as a whole person.

Maybe also she would actually say that she was now much more than a whole person The way that I experience her, is that she has much more access to her heart and her emotional life. She can laugh more easily about most things. She isn't involved in relationships that are dishonest, where she had no hope of ever getting her needs met. She now has healthier boundaries and doesn't keep dysfunctional relationships in her life.

By accepting the missing parts and learning to love them, she was able to achieve full integration of all the 'history holders' that she met, and there were many during her time in therapy.

A Spiritual Seeker.

I have worked recently with a client who would describe himself as a spiritual seeker; he had a strong faith which was very important to him and he experienced a lot of ritual and joy within this faith. He was focussed on the path of Bhakti which is the Hindu path of faith, love and devotion to a personal God. Or, in other words, the devotion to a Guru to experience divine love and reach enlightenment. This spiritual teacher has helped him immensely on his spiritual journey, and her guidance and support were helpful not only to his spiritual development but also to his damaged psyche.

He told me, though, that lately, she had become more probing about his life, because he aspired to be a good and loving person, but he appeared to her to be somewhat stuck in many ways. Eventually she told him that he should seek help to find out about his inner child, who she believed to be very damaged.

He first told me about being stuck mostly in relationships; he was unsure about how to be close to people. In one relationship, he talked about being a really good stepfather and feeling loving towards the children he was helping to bring up, but he had also realised at the same time that he was unable to accept love from others.

The more he told me about his life, there emerged a picture of someone who desperately wanted to be able to connect and experience the love that he was freely able to give to others. There was no pretending to be loving from this man and It was very clear to me that he was actually in touch with a very powerful source of love, which shone out from him, especially when he talked about the help and love he had been freely given by his Guru.

However, I could see that this divine love that he so obviously possessed, seemed to be blocked when it came to reaching his inner child and it was here that he felt stuck. Having been a spiritual seeker most of my adult life, I understood his longing for connection and the bliss that divine love can bring, but I also understood what I have said here many times, if the love, wherever it comes from, does not include the closed off parts of us, it is not complete.

I told him this, and he said he understood what I was saying, but there was no relief in my words, and I could tell that although he understood them, he did not know what they meant for him.

When the work moved on to talk about his childhood, he revealed a story of neglect, shame, poverty and hopelessness. I experienced great sadness for his inner child and I thought that it wasn't going to be easy for him to allow this part to be acknowledged; he had spent so long pushing it away that he appeared to have developed a real 'stuckness' inside.

He told me that he had no idea how to do what I was suggesting; he said that his biggest fear was "that if he really got in touch with his pain, he would cry forever".

I told him that this was so obviously the child speaking because 'forever' is a childlike word to use in this context, and that I disagreed and that he would probably cry, but not forever. He has a great sense of humour, and he found this very funny.

But in all seriousness, he still believed that he had no idea how to love or even like this boy who was trapped inside and covered with shame about his past.

In my my work, I always like to point out people's own strength so that it can be utilised to help to solve the problems. So I reminded him that he was a father and I asked if it was true that he could show these children love. He agreed that it was true.

I also reminded that he was a spiritual seeker and that he had followed the path of Bhakti and experienced God's divine love within that spiritual path? He agreed that this was true.

Then I explained to him, that his job was not to go seeking for love outside of himself, because he already had a dynamic, lived experience of love. His task was to turn the light of his own loving awareness, onto himself and especially onto his own abandoned and desperately lonely little boy. Upon hearing this, he began to cry softly.

But then suddenly and without warning, he burst into tears of laughter, "what! is it really that easy?" It was as if he couldn't believe the simple truth that I was explaining to him. He had come across what I understand as a 'cosmic' joke. It is that moment when we realise a great truth, and that truth sets us free; it's a very strange and funny moment to see through the illusion of what we previously thought to be reality.

Now, of course, it isn't that easy, his has been a lifetime of repression and rejection of his hurt self, but the 'seeing' of the problem is easy; you only have to be honest and to know what is needed is loving kindness towards yourself. This is not easy, but it is the simple truth.

These days he continues with this work, with as much passion as he felt when following his Guru and I think that if he were to offer himself just half of the love he has for her and for God, then his whole life could be immediately transformed and I do believe that it will be.

He now spends time writing and listening to his inner child's voice. He understands where it comes from and because of that he is so much kinder to himself. He was delighted that he had so easily managed to make the beginnings of a connection with the most ignored and lonely aspect of himself.

He told me a lovely little story recently. He had gone out to buy the new notebook to start his writing, and when he found the right book, he felt very happy that his 'child' had definitely chosen it.

Also in the shop, he saw a crossword book, and he was strangely drawn to it. He didn't do crosswords and had no interest in them, but he told me that he remembered that when he was a child, he sometimes noticed crossword books in other people's homes, but there were no crossword books in his house. He then let himself know the important metaphor in this message, which was, that it seemed to him that the happier houses contained crossword books, whereas in his house, there were none.

These kinds of intuitive insights come when we start to do this work, and I believe that this client is determined to offer his greatest love to his inner child, however hard it may sometimes be.

I often think of myself as great champion of the inner child, I fight for its right to exist and I become excited for a client to finally meet his younger self, not in anger or frustration, not in hatred and dread. But in gentleness, humility, strength and love where true and lasting peace lies.

Nine

Hiding in plain sight

The birds they sing, at the break of day

Start again, I heard them say

Don't dwell on what has passed away

Or what is yet to be

Ah the wars they will be fought again, the holy dove she will be caught again

Bought and sold and bought again, the dove is never free

Ring the bells that still can ring, forget your perfect offering

There is a crack in everything

That's how the light gets in.

Song: Anthem

Artist: Leonard Cohen

Album: The Future 1992

Background

I was born into a working-class family in the north of England. My father was a sailor in the Royal Navy, with very high standards for others but very low requirements of himself.

My mother had been looking after her father and her younger twin brother and sister since her own mother abandoned her when she was fourteen, leaving her to figure it out for herself. She met my father when she was nineteen, and maybe they fell in love.

Whether they did or not, I have no way of knowing now, but what is known to me was that my mother became pregnant, and my father immediately ran away from England. He managed to arrange for the navy to send him to Australia, where he stayed for three years.

My mum and I lived in my grandad's home, and I was well cared for by my wonderful grandfather, my young aunt and uncle and my sometimes happy mother.

My dad must have had a change of heart because he decided to return to England and take up his responsibilities, and asked my mother to marry him. Sounds like a happy ending? It really wasn't, though, because his abandonment of her had already caused her great shame and pain, and even though she wanted to say no to his proposal, she said yes. She admitted to me many years later, near the end of her life, that she had married him to punish him.

I already knew this, and I think I knew it from a very early age. I also knew that our family was flawed and built on a lie. Both of my parents had difficult childhoods, and so I don't believe that coming together in the way that they did was an accident.

They found each other, one to angrily withhold and one to drink and gamble compulsively, a perfect storm of dysfunction and the typically co-dependent family.

It was inevitable that both my brother and I would also experience a difficult childhood. I think I am just setting up a bare minimum of a stage so that there is some understanding of how the actors in this story played out their parts. Because this is not a memoir or a biography, it is my experience of a life-changing event and, as such, has some insights into why I was riddled with obsessions, a lack of security, abandonment fears, not much self-esteem, and a great fear of life. These feelings continued far too long, but I know that for some, this kind of childhood is never understood or resolved, and someone one can live a life that is sometimes ok but often contains the shadows of the past, and some actions are never understood.

Alcohol became attractive to me, my dad drank to excess and he always seemed happier when he was drunk. He was the kind of drunk that no one ever saw as a drunk; he never fell over and, he never looked drunken. He was someone who could hold his drink well, it could be said.

It is interesting to me now that I only noticed that he looked happy when he drank, and I completely ignored the reality of his life and, therefore, of ours. He was violent to my mother; he was a very angry man when drunk, and he was an obsessive gambler whose whole life was built on winning or losing. The truth was that my dad was a sad mess, and he would never admit this, and he never did.

So ignoring all of these warning signs, I stumbled into drinking when I was fourteen, and I realised what it could do for me from the beginning. I found life difficult, and drinking helped me not be too stressed, anxious, or shy. I found emotions difficult, and drinking helped me to bury them. I found relationships difficult, and when I was drunk, I didn't care about them. I found the understanding of myself the most difficult, and when I was drunk, I found it easier not to expect anything from myself. I expected so little that I turned then to using stronger substances to escape even deeper from a reality that I had decided I did not like, and a life of drug abuse then also ran alongside my bad drinking habits.

I believe now that although addiction is not formed in childhood events, the propensity for choosing alcohol as a solution to emotional problems does have a link. It was certainly taught to me in my childhood that the drinker avoids the feelings, and the 'other' carries all the problems, pain, and responsibility. I did not want to be the 'other' like my mother. I definitely wanted to be the one who could escape and run away into addictions.

I came from a dysfunctional family, and through no one's fault, I followed this codependent and dysfunctional life myself. It seemed inevitable.

The lifestyle

This lifestyle started in the mid-sixties when I was just 14, and during this time, I would take any drug that came my way, and I also continued to abuse alcohol consistently. I became a mother to two children in the late 60s and early 70s, and I would love to say that this stopped my addiction, but it did not. I carried on with even more guilt and shame, and this is the perfect story of addiction. The more you use, the less good you feel about yourself because addiction is not only a killer, but it is also a thief of everything that is good in life.

I gave birth to another child when I was thirty, and my decision to have this child came because I had loved the feeling when I had been pregnant with my two other children. I had felt happy and whole, and I felt as if I had a wonderful purpose in life, which was to be a mother; I wanted this feeling again.

The only story I am telling here is that drinking and using drugs became a terrible way of life for me, and I continued to use this method of running away from myself and those who needed and loved me until I was thirty-two.

Then I stopped.

I stopped because of these children who had all suffered from my lifestyle each in their own way.

I stopped for them and for no other reason at that time, later I would continue recovery for my own needs.

This was my first spiritual awakening, which I did not recognise until much later. In those years of using I became a God hater, an anti-social rebel, and a committed socialist. I had a lot of ideas and no way to fulfil them. I was someone who wanted to do so much more in life but failed to do anything but fail.

So my only spiritual insight was that I could never hurt my children again, ever.

I began to change from this point on the 4th of June, 1985

The change

I started to make the changes needed with the help and support of 12-step fellowships. These fellowships have been invaluable to my process, and I do believe that I couldn't have achieved anywhere near as much change as I have over the past thirty-seven years without the help and guidance that I found there. 12-step fellowship became the solid ground on which I was able to stand up and be a responsible human being. I gained skills that I never had before. I began to understand my impulses and my needs. I became employable.

All of these external things began to make life easier, and in a relatively short time, I was physically stronger and much healthier. I was emotionally recovering and discovering new ways of relating to people. By being employable, I was able to earn money, and I became financially better Life moved on, and before long, I had a degree in Social Work. This was something amazing to me as I had an internal voice that continued to tell me that I was stupid, and I completely believed it.

What I continued to struggle with was my mental health. I still had poor impulse control, no way of soothing myself, and I still could get lost in self-hatred. I remained very codependent for a long time into my recovery, even though I continued to do what was suggested to me to maintain a sober life.

I had been an avid reader from a young age, and as I grew up, I then became fixated on the self-help genre. I read so many and so often, and I loved the idea that reading was not only escapism and fantasy. But it was possible to understand myself more clearly through listening to writers who had changed themselves and learned from the process, then offering these hard-won insights into the human condition.

Around the mid-nineties, I read many books on codependency, and they seemed to be able to answer some more of my internal struggles. I came across a writer, Robert Burney, who had just published his book, The Dance of the Wounded Souls, in 1996, and it had a great impact on me because I found that his explanations and stories fit with my experience, and I think I began to understand my family more. I also read Melody Beaty's Co-dependent no more and Robin Norwood's excellent book, which talked about women who loved too much, I didn't hold out much hope for this book as I didn't consider myself a woman who loved too much, but I thought of myself as a woman who didn't love enough! I was surprised then to find my codependent self exactly in the pages of her book. I was then able to fully accept that I was a codependent woman and my object of fixation was on men who I thought could heal me or take care of me.

Not all of these relationships were bad; some were really good in many different ways, not least helping me to learn more about myself within the relationship. Until they ended, as they inevitably did, I had not developed any of the skills needed to be in a long-term relationship. I had no softness or forgiveness, no great communication skills, and I was so easily triggered into shame, confusion, and anger from an inner child that I had now heard of but was still mostly unaware of how it operated in my life and what a powerful force it wielded.

Psychotherapy training

In 2001 I had the good fortune to enter psychotherapy training, and my understanding of my processes was accelerated. A trainee therapist has to have at least 40 hours per year of therapy for herself, and I found this incredibly daunting, despite having been in recovery for many years, I was still scared of what I might find out about myself in therapy. I resonated with this saying;

I want to be an open book, but I don't want to open the pages.

I don't know who said this, but it seemed like a perfect description of me at this time. But what I did know was that there were definitely parts of myself that were holding me back from success, from peace of mind, from connection with others, and although at that time I had no idea what these things were or how they could be helped, but I was ready.

Being ready is a wonderful opportunity. I was ready enough to attempt the task of taking a hard look at my life for the second time and delving into the subconscious to discover what was locked away in the basement of my psyche

For me, what I particularly found in the basement was an inner child that was so unhappy. I believed that I would cry forever if I allowed myself the space. I have certainly sat with many clients who had this same fear that if they really opened up and faced what they were most frightened to face, they would never stop crying.

In fact, I did do a lot of crying, but it certainly was not anywhere near forever. This is an inner child's fear response; it's so obviously 'child's speak.' Forever is a complete exaggeration about anything in life, nothing lasts forever, but the inner child has a tendency to talk in this manner.

This seemed like a new awareness to be able to look at the language I used and to begin to see the 'child speaking' voice. I kept notes, and I discovered that the voices inside my head were very harsh and critical and were out of proportion to what was happening in my life. I was clean and sober, and I was making a good life for myself. I had completed four years at university, I was helpful to others and loving to my family. I was embarking on this career change that was to have so many extra benefits to me than that of getting a qualification.

But in spite of these wonderful things happening to me, my internal voice still insisted that I was a loser, that I would never amount to anything, and that I was still stupid and always had been. When I delved a bit further, I could even see times when my 'thought talk' had been absolutely hateful towards me, the choices I made, and the actions I took. This voice did not like me one little bit; she actively seemed to hate me.

When I began this work that I was indeed ready to do, I thought it would be as simple as stopping saying these awful words to myself; that if I was kinder in the words that I chose, I would automatically feel better. But what I didn't know then was that this is not just a case of the language we use to talk to ourselves, but it is absolutely spoken by someone else who I have no control over; and the language I was trying to change was not within my power to change!

This was a shock to me, and it was to involve digging deeper into my past, which gave me clues as to why these particular voices spoke to me in the way that they did. I reached into parts of me that were very painful to feel again, but I have to say that they were not nearly as painful as I had imagined. I had discovered the wonderful truth, which is that a healing process is a way out of something; it is not the same as sitting with feelings alone with no direction and feeling them over and over again, this is pain that leads nowhere, and the other is pain that moves us to a different place. In other words, healing ourselves brings about a change, which then begins to feel different and replaces old worn-out scripts.

The healing

I was one of those people who knew that my childhood was difficult. There were two things that were the main threads of both my childhood and my adult life. One was a defence, and the other was a cause.

1. That If I were to be safe in life, then I believed that it was completely down to me to 'be strong,' and this way of being became my life to a ridiculous degree. I never showed anyone my fear. I acted as if I had none. I never asked anyone for help, it was outside of my experience, and the idea that I could never occurred to me. I used this harsh way of being in the world to always reject my ideas and beliefs, and I alienated any part of myself that could help me. The trap of 'be strong' is very debilitating and exhausting and offers no other way out except to just keep going because that is the nature of a be strong driver, just carry on and don't allow anyone to see the cracks.

2. The loudest of my internal voices was, without any doubt, that of my mother. She had suffered from neglect and rejection, and she was internally self-hating. She also carried a be strong driver, and she was stoic and very strong; I was no match for her. I believe that she projected this hatred of herself onto me in that she didn't really like me, and I felt it. I think that when I became an adult, and especially an adult in recovery, she changed a towards me, and we did manage to have a really beautiful relationship, but she still remained

judgemental and harsh with her words to both herself and others.

My mother's rejection of herself became my rejection of myself, and I am guessing that it was also my grandmother's way and her mother's way too. The voice of my mother was split off in the way I have described, and it did not seem to belong to anyone but me. It spoke to me as if it were a part of me that was also a judge of me and all of my actions.

It had always seemed to me to be a watcher and critic who observed everything that I did or said and approved of absolutely none of it. As a child, my mother's dislike of us both came out mostly in judgement, unkindness, cruelty, and rage, and I spent most of my childhood in fear.

My inner voices disliked the way I spoke, disliked the things I did, disliked my clothing, disliked my choices, it seemed to dislike everything about me, and all of these patterns came directly from my poor mum, who hated herself so much.

I began to understand how my inner child was born, where she came from, and why she had to split off parts of her difficulties. I cannot say that the work was easy because it was not. It was painful to follow the thread back and view my developing child self from a kinder viewpoint instead of the harshness that I had manufactured in order to help me to survive. It was difficult to catch myself using harsh language and changing it to kinder words. But by far, the most difficult part was to find the compassion needed to begin to like myself.

The voice that spoke to me for all of my life, in a nasty, judgmental way, was the most difficult thing for me to change because I absolutely believed its belief that I was bad, unlovable, and evil sometimes. It was difficult to see it for what it was, and it was definitely a 'not me' part of me. I could see that I was not one whole being and that there were other parts of me that held opposing thoughts, feelings, and beliefs. This was such a revelation and after getting used to the idea, it began to make so much sense, and not only did it make cognitive sense, but it felt true and mirrored my experience. This understanding then also helped me to trust in my own experience, which I have never felt able to do previously.

This was the start of another great change in my life, and I felt determined to understand, to change what could from the place that I was at, to be kind and loving towards not only my adult self but also to the frightened little girl who had lived in trauma for years. One of the most astounding truths that I discovered was that my child self was lonely because I perpetuated her loneliness by ignoring, running away, rejecting, and speaking unkindly to myself. Then it became that every day, every week, and every year of continuing the essence of this work, another truth emerged, and that was that we could put ourselves in the position of thriving instead of merely surviving.

Present time.

I want to end this chapter with a short story about something that happened to me last year, and, I think, illustrates the ongoing nature of this kind of healing.

When I conceived the idea of writing this book, it was over five years ago, and then only in short bursts of putting it down over and over again. I could not find my authentic voice; I became pompous and sounded as if I was talking down to the reader. I was completely stuck in what I thought was writer's block.

During some time in the previous months, I had attended a workshop with Robert Burney, which I had enjoyed very much. Robert had offered counselling sessions to the participants at a very low cost, and I thought that I would have some counselling with him and try to discover what the blockage was. Because I thought that I had a lot of experience in the subject, I thought I had something new to add. I believed I had a good perspective as not only someone who had done a lot of inner work but had also worked with others in groups and one-to-one therapy, to guide them on the way to their own healing. Why could I not then write this book?

So I arranged a session with Robert online, and we spoke together about how writing a book can bring up fears that had previously worked on. That it was exposing to write a book as I had discovered, and that I couldn't find my voice and I was using my ego as a defence mechanism.

Robert said at the end of our session, *"you know what, Sue, maybe you don't have a book to write, maybe you don't really want to? How would it be to not write this book?"* He asked me to think about these ideas, why I was writing, where I was stuck, and to see if anything came up when doing some meditation, journalling, and sitting with the idea of finishing this book.

So I did this, I meditated and thought of the conversations we'd had, I journaled, and wrote questions and listened for the answers. I was focused because I really wanted to know what was stopping me. After all of this counselling, preparation, writing, meditating, and listening, I received an answer to the question, "Why am I not finishing this book?" The answer came directly from my inner child:

"Why would someone read a book by a little nothing like you?"

Stunned silence from me.

I was completely shocked that this voice could still be there, still vitriolic, still nasty, and still too frightened to show herself to the world.

It made me feel sad and caused me to turn away, not wanting to expose myself by writing and putting it out into the world for the world to judge. This is an old fear of mine, the judgement of others, still held onto by this 'teenager' inside and said to me at times of stress.

But I have given myself years of discovering and healing all of the various characters inside, and after the initial sadness, I could hear the voice and respond to it with kindness. I was then able to acknowledge her fear and uncomfortableness in the writing process. I told her I was sorry that she still felt fear about showing herself and her vulnerability. I listened to her, took her fear seriously, and then offered her some loving kindness. I told her that I think I do have a book to write and that she shouldn't worry about this because it is my decision, and I will be the writer, not her. I will be the one to take the judgement if it comes because I am the adult who can face all of what life throws at me, who can take risks, who can forgive, let go of things that don't serve me, and so many more skills that I can now fully recognise. Unlike before, when I found it impossible to accept my flawed sense of self.

She seemed ok with this solution, and she has calmed down again now lets me just get on with it. I often wonder whether we can ever completely claim back these 'parts' of ourselves, or do they continue to think their own thoughts and have their own 'life' in a more or less separate way?

Sometimes these days, as I am writing, and I become a bit stuck or reluctant to sit down at my desk, I can hear her saying some encouragement or bringing up a disagreement about the work with me. Once when I was reassuring myself that what

I was writing was actually ok, I heard just the softest sound of "hmmm," which sounded to me, just like a teenager who still thinks I'm a bit flakey.

I do believe that this aspect of me is still there, she is still quite vocal, but I like to think that she is fairly happy living with me now. We get along pretty well as long as I'm attentive and loving towards her, and why would I not be?

I have discovered that she is a part of my soul, the keeper of my pain, and she completes me.

Ten

The exact nature of this work.

Some say love, it is a river. That drowns the
tender reed

Some say love, it is a razor. That leaves your
soul to bleed

Some say love, it is a hunger. An endless aching
need

I say love, it is a flower. And you its only seed

It's the heart, afraid of breaking. That never
learns to dance

It's the dream, afraid of waking. That never
takes the chance

It's the one who won't be taken. Who cannot
seem to give

And the soul afraid of dying

That never learns to live.

Song: The Rose

Album: The Rose

Artist: Bette Midler 1979

One of the most effective ways to make lasting change in your life is to recognise your negative inner self-talk, which is the inner dialogue that interferes with your ability to believe in yourself and your capabilities. There is a great need to listen to these inner voices, to know what they sound like, and what they are saying to you.

I also believe that bringing anything into our awareness is a profound aspect of change and healing. Make notes that help you to build this awareness. Vigilance is needed to stop their whisperings, before they can take hold of your thinking and drag you into some very dark places over and over again.

Understanding is needed to discover where these negative voices originate from and how they exist in your mind. Why do you listen to them? Why do you think that they are in charge of you? Your freedom comes from liberation from your own negative feedback and you then become the master of your own destiny. It is you who can decide what your future is going to be, how you will respond to others, which information you will base your actions on and how you will make beneficial choices. You will have a newfound internal strength to make your own uncontaminated decisions about your life.

Our thought voices are the beliefs and fears of our traumatised inner child; just let that sink in for a moment.

What this means is that it is our traumatised self that makes the decisions about how we are going to face life, how we are going to live, love, work, and even enjoy this life.

Doesn't it seem wrong to allow a child to make these far-reaching assumptions and decisions about our adult life? It is not the fault of the child, nor is the fault of the adult; it is a consequence of a trauma response in a child.

This has far-reaching implications for us if the child's beliefs are heard by us and assumed to be our beliefs, as they usually are, due to them being deeply imprinted in our mind memories and in our bodily memory.

We think that these beliefs are ours because we haven't realised until now that we are not one unified person but have many split-off versions of ourselves, who were most likely to have been traumatised at different times and therefore were of different ages and held differing beliefs than each other.

These are some examples of the underlying beliefs of the child and the probable consequences of them:

- A belief that no one is trustworthy. Then as adults, we believe that all people are untrustworthy and that we will not trust anyone fully. We may learn a bit about trust and know cognitively that its' a really good thing to have in relationships, but it seems almost impossible to do. Maybe in some cases or in some relationships, trust is easier to develop, but generally, there will be mistrust in others that is evident to see and feel. This is especially true in love relationships, where mistrust can completely destroy a good connection. Within the belief that people are untrustworthy, there will most likely be feelings of jealousy, anger, suspicion, intolerance, and self-doubt.

- A belief that life is difficult and/or cruel, and with this belief in adulthood, we find life a struggle, our expectations are lowered, and we often don't ask for help because it seems as if it is our particular load to carry and no one else can understand it. The feelings that come from this belief could be self-pity, isolation, sadness, hopelessness, and many more.

- A belief that no one cares about us is a common one for the inner child to have. The adult then believes that if this feels true, therefore, it is true.

- When we find ourselves in situations where if we have been excluded for any reason, it

110

then becomes part of the story that no one cares about us. It's sad because it was probably either because carers did not 'care' well enough for many different reasons or that they didn't care enough in some very important times and many other possibilities.

- A belief that you are unlovable Stems from some of the ways you were treated physically, emotionally, or physically. You were not given enough kind nurturing, not enough positive verbal affirmations. Possibly hurt and neglected physically. This belief can be deeply held where no other information from the present is allowed to get inside, and we cling on to it as if it is the actual truth.

- A belief that you will always fail is often born out of doing your very best and then being tormented by carers for not doing better. There are many other events that could have their roots in the reasons why we underachieve, not being happy at home, for so many reasons, can't focus due to worries and no one to share them with. It could also be made out of having parents who are overachievers and have too high expectations of children. Whatever the cause, this belief is undoubtedly a heavy burden.

These are examples of the kind of decisions about life that we make as children and carry into adult life. I have not described too many examples of the traumas that could cause each belief because I think that any belief could correlate with any trauma. It may even be that a cumulative trauma would have most, if not all, of these beliefs attached to it, therefore becoming more complex to deal with and to discover the source of.

We bear this in mind when we are searching to discover the childhood beliefs that we hold about life when we go into this written work.

Eleven

These are the steps

The Journey of a thousand miles, begins with one step.

These are the steps that I have used to guide you through the maze that is the healing of the inner child. I have used steps because I love them, as I've already told you in my story. So to write guidelines as steps to be able to achieve something makes perfect sense to me. It also suits my slightly autistic process in that I always like to know which step I'm working on.

They go from 1 to 6, so therefore there are not too many, but enough to delineate the changing of each one and, to my mind anyway, make them seem linear, which is exactly the way they are written, actually, but the process of healing is not linear.

I think of it these days as a spiral, and once we have done the first round of the spiral, we find ourselves back at the beginning. But we don't recognise it as the beginning because, by the time we have made the first loop, we have changed, even if only a little bit, and thus as changed people, we forget exactly how we were, when we started.

I remember when I started on the healing journey, I would find myself facing something again that looked almost exactly like something that I had previously faced, and I would say to myself, "Bloody hell, I thought I knew that. How the hell did I land up back here again?" It was many years later that I discovered this idea of a spiral as a path, and this one small piece of knowledge was so helpful to me. It meant that I didn't have to beat myself up when it happened again because some things are so deeply and painfully held that only by seeing them from different angles, with a clearer understanding would we be able to handle them at all.

So follow the steps in your own time, and if you find yourself back doing something that you have done before, remember the image of the spiral and know that you are with something deeply rooted and probably therefore, more painful. Be kind to yourself in the process.....always.

Step One

Information & Knowledge

"You can't heal it until you can feel it."

This first step is having read this book, you now have some more information about what the problem is, why it is happening, and what it means to you. You will have understood the areas I have been focusing on in all of the ways that I have said the same thing. So through repetition, you will now have a clearer understanding of where your painful parts might live, in which stories they dwell and in which memories they exist. You will also have read the theory behind what I have been suggesting to you along the way, and this will give you more knowledge about how we abandon those parts of us that are in desperate need of love and care.

You may have decided to do a bit more research; you may look up a few ideas that have been mentioned here. You may want a bit more information about processes of change, shame, or the inner child. You will have had thoughts and feelings while reading this book because it is an emotional journey to find your inner child, and it is a difficult journey and not for the faint-hearted.

Maybe though, you have got to the point where you have done all of these things in search of your solution to the problem. The question of what is wrong with me can have many answers: Are my problems based on shame? Is it that I have a poor self-image? Is it because of my childhood and the things that I don't like to remember? Is it because I really am as crazy as I think I am? Is it because all of my relationships eventually fall apart? Is it that I never know the next right thing to do? Is it because I feel lost and alone? Is it because I feel sad most of the time?

If the answer is YES to all of these questions, then the answer must be the healing of your inner child because this aspect of us can cause so much havoc within our minds, emotions, and bodies in the present.

It is exactly the right time for you to be looking for this solution, reading about it, and trying to do something about this awful question "what is wrong with me?" And even in this question are the beginnings of change. If we can ask the question and allow it to really be a question, then there is always the possibility of there being an answer.

We don't usually buy a self-help book with the intention of not reading it or taking any notice of its suggestions. But sometimes, we do exactly that. We buy a new non-fiction self-help book because we want to know something specific about what we are currently concerned about.

I have bought so many books that I believed would give me some wisdom that I currently lacked. Full of excitement to open the book and start the process; maybe it starts off well, and I instantly love the writer's style, but there is something else that draws me in. I am still a bit nervous because I have lost interest in so many books over the years and my shelves are littered with books only partially read.

Sometimes the writer loses me because he approaches the subject from an angle I wasn't expecting. Sometimes I get bored and find the book too repetitious. Sometimes I realise that it's too theoretical to be enjoyable, and I sometimes reluctantly put it down, maybe to be picked up later. I would conservatively say that out of 20 self-help books that I have bought recently, I have read around 7 to the end and enjoyed them. So it shows me that not all will appeal to me, even in the specific category I like, and I also like the genre to be very specific about what it is talking about and who it will appeal to.

So I am assuming here that you have read through the previous 70 pages and discovered that this book could give you useful and usable information, enough to make you stick with it so far. Or maybe you've just got more stickability than me?

But what I am saying is that information gathering, and a certain amount of knowledge is what's needed as a base to discovering more about almost any new venture.

Step 2

Making Contact

This second step is where you make contact with your inner child, and you start to put some action into this work, not just reading or listening. It is time to do something instead of thinking about doing things. I am suggesting at this point that you start to keep a journal.

My experience tells me that this step must start the process with action, as we can get lost in the mind, and change happens in what we do differently, not what we consider doing.

So this first act of doing is to go shopping. Shopping to find yourself the kind of notebook that appeals to the child within. You are making a new start, and this is something you may not have done for yourself before. It is always a good idea to make this initial connection with the lost inner child part of you more real from the start. You may not know how to do this, and I want you to use your imagination to help you to envisage an image of yourself from when you were young; any age between 4 and 8 would be good. This is who you are taking with you on this day out, it may feel strange to you at first, but if you suspend your scepticism, you may find that something different happens to what you expected.

You can speak to him and tell him that you are going to buy this notebook because you want to discover more about him and that you would like

119

him to come with you. This is very likely the first invite that he has ever had from you; it may surprise him. Because the only time previously that there has been communication has been when you've had to deal with those difficult triggers, that are, the difficult emotions of sadness, anger, or resentment. This is exactly how he has been communicating his feelings to you for all of your adult life; this is what 'acting out' looks like.

There is a great deal written about when you want to make changes to your thoughts, habits, patterns, etc., that it is done from a calm space within and not a difficult place. It is impossible to look objectively at your behaviours when you are flooded by neurochemicals in the brain, which affect moods, emotions, and hormones, so you are in an altered state and usually have high arousal. This writing can only really be done when you are more calm and settled and in a position to look at the triggers that preceded your acting-out behaviours. Our triggers are the clues to discovering our weak spots and, therefore, our trauma pain.

Even if it feels as if it is only in your imagination that you are talking to the inner child, so what? Imagination is a wonderful thing and very useful in all sorts of situations. In metaphor, stories, fables, analogies, mind over matter, the power of positive thinking, affirmations, etc. I have found that the average mind is not as clever as it believes itself to be.

We use imagination in many ways, and I think that it's a good idea to suspend our scepticism in this cause. We will begin to understand and believe more as we see changes begin to happen. Understanding and experience comes from doing something, not from not doing something.

The beauty of inner child work is that this child lives inside you and has been watching you and listening to you for most of your life. They hear everything that is said, thought, or acted upon. They know exactly how you feel about them, whether you love them or whether you are always looking for ways to get rid of them. Even this 'healing' can be seen as a way to get rid of the inner child and never have to be bothered with them again, which is what most clients want to do. Even if they don't say it in a bad way, what they usually mean is, let's get this work done as soon as possible, then I won't be bothered by these problems in my life, and I will feel happier.

The buying of the notebook may seem like such a simple step, but it is much more than that; it is possibly, and for many people, the first contact ever with their inner child. Now I think that this is pretty bloody amazing! Just to start such a conversation is the very essence of beginning any relationship; we say hello….

So in this way, you introduce yourselves to the inner child. You use simple language and are always trying to be honest in your communications. You tell him that you have just become aware of his existence and that you are ready to get to know who he is.

Isn't this just how you would speak to a child that you have just met for the first time? Isn't it natural to be softer speaking, polite, willing to listen, and wanting to understand more? If this isn't coming naturally to you, then maybe you have a bit more research to do.

Step 3

Discovery

This third step is the part of the work that seems the most difficult to people. What am I looking for? What do I write about? What should I say?

But let me try to break it down and discover more of what you are trying to do here. You have understood about change being necessary for growth. You have seen how the inner child has become something that people understand more, study, and hopefully interact with in order to achieve changes. You have seen the kind of situations that give rise to the birth of the inner child, codependency and shame, family dysfunction, addictions, loss, death, emotional neglect, and abusive events of many kinds. You have information on how and why we split off parts of ourselves. You have read about other people who have discovered that by trying to do this work, often there can be a kind of awakening, a moment of aha, I see what I have been doing.

Here you are, with all of this information, and with the burning question, "what do I do next?"

The answer?......You start one of the most healing modalities known, and you write. You write about what you already know from your childhood so that you can understand where your most painful memories lie, where your triggers are likely to be and what memories keep replaying in your mind. In stories, in pictures, in memory, when you see your parents when you look at old photographs, and in fact, in any way that the information comes to you.

As mentioned earlier, you may have strong and clear memories, or you may have suppressed your memory unconsciously or purposefully. But here is the space to write a story about the parts of your childhood that were difficult in some way. There may only be a few memories available to you, there may be very many, and every one of them is probably painful.

You are not writing this story to hurt yourself, you are not telling it to feel sorry for yourself, and you're not going to blame anyone for it. You are going to write a short story about the things that happened to you and that you felt some pain about. I ask you to keep it short, not fall into too many feelings, and do not dwell on the story. This is an exercise, and it needs to be written by your adult self.

Let me remind you of what adults do. They work things out; they can be logical, they understand, they survive, they have many life skills, they are able to think things through, and they make good and bad decisions. We are a mixture of good and bad, difficult and simple, unhealthy patterns and healthy patterns. Everything has an opposite, and in everything we think we are, we can always find the opposite. This perspective is a good way to look at ourselves and not from a black-and-white place of judgement. All human beings are deeply flawed, and that really is OK.

So you call on your adult to take a view of the events of your past in the most dispassionate way you possibly can. If there are tears and sadness with these stories, feel those emotions and then move on as soon as you are able. Not to push them away but to allow the feelings to come, but not to overtake you in this task.

There will be more tears later, it's inevitable that there are tears, but I know that there can be tears of healing when you really get to understanding who it is that you are trying to help.

But for now, this is your current task; you are writing about your childhood from your adult perspective. All I would ask to help you in this task is that you are kinder to yourself than you have ever thought of being.

It doesn't have to be perfect writing or use good grammar, it is only for your eyes, and as such, it needn't have to please anyone else. Some of it may even be written in child-like scrawl, and that, too, is ok.

You're doing this for your benefit, and it is important that you're not hard on yourself at any point. If you notice that your inner voice is being a bit harsh or using judgemental words, please just ask it nicely not to speak to you like that.

One of the aspects of doing this work is that you do begin to realise that you are not just one unified person but, in fact, are made up of very different parts which all have their own thoughts, belief systems, and ideas. It can be very freeing to see ourselves like this. We have mixed sub-personalities, and we can talk to them as separate from us. Trust me when I say that this helps.

Step 4

Triggers

This step is where you do something each day to make your process much clearer, and this is what you will have written up to now:

•   You have written a short story of your life as a child.

•   You have seen the parts of your childhood that were more difficult than others.

•   You have written about the parts that were traumatic.

•   You have allowed yourself to accept these difficult traumas as true.

Well done. It is never easy to face up to the reality of unacceptable truths because it is painful to know that your childhood was hard at times. But that knowledge is not nearly as difficult as you imagine; you are working through something, changing ideas that have become stuck, you are freeing yourself, and rejoining with a long-abandoned part of you.

I think you probably know where your trigger points are already. Let me give you another clue. The triggers will come from the times when there has been stress in your childhood experiences. The triggers for your adult self are in the here and now and are linked to these past experiences.

Step 4 then is about watching for these triggers and, when they come, learning something new from them. It is a habit that we do not see the links to our past experiences that are still controlling our present.

What makes this not an easy thing to do is that triggers come hurtling through us, powered by strong emotions. They are hard to understand, and difficult to control, and they always take us by surprise. The reason for this is that triggers usually, but not always, come from the people who we are in contact with. The closer the relationship, the bigger the trigger.

A story about triggers.

Here is the scene.

Sophie is at a dinner party with her partner Mick and some friends. The evening has been going well, and Sophie is feeling happy and relaxed. Mick decides to have a bit of fun with Sophie, it's okay they often have banter between them, and it's just fun, isn't it?

But this night is feeling a bit different to Sophie; her shoulders are tense, and she notices that she feels hot, flushed, and is feeling a bit scared for no apparent reason. Mick is laughing at some joke that's been made; you hear him say to no one in particular and everyone in the room. "Well, Sophie would never do that; she's always too scared, frightened of her own shadow. Sophie's a real baby."

She feels her jaw clench, her stomach knots, tears sting her eyes, and she feels compelled to run from the room. But she doesn't run; she remains sitting and smiling, looking composed with a smile that is passed onto her face. She knows that she's not convincing anyone but still doesn't move and doesn't say anything. She just continues to sit as still as she can and feeling terrible.

Then her internal voice speaks to her, "I knew that Mick was a prick' you can't half pick 'em," what you are you gonna do now? Run away as usual. Mick's right; you are a total baby."

Sophie has no idea what's going on now, but she is beginning to feel trapped and a bit foolish, and she is flooded by feelings that she cannot understand. She notices that everyone is laughing, and the focus is still on her. Mick has cracked another 'joke,' and he seems to be on a roll now. "Oh, Sophie doesn't mind; she's always good for a laugh, aren't you, Sophie?"

It's just at this exact moment that the easygoing, good-for-a-laugh Sophie stands up, and throws the beer she's been holding right into Mick's face, and runs out of the room.

Mick is shocked, and so are their friends.

We will leave Sophie and Mick now; maybe they patch things up, maybe they don't, and maybe they carry on the resentment for a long time without any understanding of what happened from either side.

Sounds familiar? It is a short story of how the inner child shows herself in the body, with uncomfortable feelings, and then speaks out in an angry manner in defence of herself. But If we knew some of Sophie's history, it may make more sense why she felt uncomfortable and angry.

Sophie's childhood was mostly happy; she had a mother and father that were good parents, who had decent jobs and earned good money. There was no lack of anything, and Sophie would have reported that her upbringing was great. But ask a few more questions, and she might tell you that her father was a bit of a tease, at least that's what he called it.

If Sophie was able to allow the full story to come into her awareness, she might tell you that her father was actually a bully and entertained himself by bullying Sophie relentlessly.

Ask some more probing questions, and she would tell you that she often thought that her father didn't love her, but that he preferred to torment her. Sophie often lay in bed crying because she couldn't understand why her dad was like this. Most of her friends thought he was a lot of fun.

Eventually, Sophie might tell you that she was very frightened of her father, who was a drinker, and there were times when he would not only bully but lose his temper, shout, and sometimes hit both of his children. But he always apologised, she would then add.

Sophie's inner child was born within this bullying atmosphere; she was constantly made the butt of her dad's jokes, laughed at, and sometimes physically hurt. Her inner child made up a belief that men are not to be trusted sometimes. She became withdrawn and scared to speak up for herself in any situation. Sophie became a people pleaser and could put up with an awful lot of 'teasing.'

When Sophie was an adult, she didn't know that this trauma, which she didn't even recognise as trauma, still lived inside her. She didn't know that she was somehow compelled to attract men who were, at best, teasers and at worst, bullies. She certainly didn't know that she had a seriously wounded inner child.

I think this story illustrates how triggers are activated and then acted out. It's almost as if the child part of us climbs into the driving seat of our emotions and just takes over, revealing the emotions of the past, which will always seem to be in the present.

It is clear that this work takes a lot of energy and commitment to be able to catch these processes, and that is what I am asking you to do in this step. It is difficult to catch yourself when you are in the middle of a triggering situation.

You can see that if Sophie had the information that you have been reading and working on, she would have had a better chance to know what was happening to her emotions.

But also, I am suggesting that the time to capture your triggers are when they are cold because when they are cold, it's easier. I mean cold as in not hot, fiery and alive, that the sting has gone out of them, we are not so emotionally caught up in the drama.

After a cooling down period when one of these triggering experiences has recently happened, this is the time to look at them. To make the connection to the physical sensations and emotional feelings that were so difficult to handle in the moment.

To allow yourself to clearly see the links from the past to the present.

Get to know yourself fully, and get to know your inner child and how she functions. What she is scared of, and what beliefs she has made out of the scare.

The trigger situations can teach us a lot of what we need to know. Triggers are pointing to our painful memories, and they are very useful to help us to steady and understand our emotional response to people in our lives and to our made-up world view.

The task of step 4 is to write about the missing link between our traumatised child and our adult self so that we can clearly know these important connections that are our direct clues to understanding the past.

Step 5

Commitment

In step five, we make a commitment to ourselves to continue with this work, it's not going to change unless we carry on. This commitment is to yourself, and you are saying to the child part of you that you have just met, I am committed to carry on seeing and hearing you.

If you do nothing else with it, it would be like promising a child a wonderful present, that she becomes very excited about it. She went with you to choose the present and saw you also being excited and writing plans for her. But after some time, sadly, this gift was never delivered. Can you imagine how disappointed this child would be?

Well, this is exactly how it is. After all her time of waiting to be noticed by you, you eventually start to speak to her and show some interest; she allows herself to hope that something will be different. But then, sadly, this action comes to nothing much, and she becomes even more lonely than she had been before you met her.

You cannot afford to ignore this aspect of yourself anymore. You are so close, and yet, what keeps you from following through with this commitment? Because commitment is what it takes to make lasting changes.

You have by now written about the trauma that you suffered as a child. You have looked at the trigger points and their connection to the child's self. You have understood that this process is happening all of the time. You know that it has been purposefully hidden from you since the day the inner child was born in you. You have felt the pain inside yourself. You have acknowledged how you have acted out in the past, in desperation, in neglect of yourself, and ran away into all kinds of dysfunctional behaviour.

So the question is, are you going to make a serious commitment to yourself? Are you serious about taking the actions that create change? Some of the thoughts that might block you sound like this.

You don't believe that you can change, so you don't bother.

You can't see how working in this way can change anything about the past, so you don't bother.

You are frightened of digging up the painful past, so you don't bother.

You would prefer to keep looking for other answers that may work so you don't bother.

You keep turning to God to help you, so you don't bother.

You feel too damaged for such a simple answer, so again, you don't bother.

These excuses are just that, fear-driven excuses. You have nothing to lose. If it doesn't work, then you can try something else. It probably will be painful, but emotional pain doesn't kill us. You will be able to find examples in your adult life when you have made and sustained a good change for yourself; remember it.

This really is not a 'maybe I will and maybe I won't decision,' it's an imperative decision.

This process has been going on since the child self was born and became a real identity living its lonely life inside of you and beside you all the way. He carried for you the pain that you were unable to carry because you were a child trying to survive.

He was the part of you that volunteered for the job; he was taking a hit for the team. But what a hit he took and I guess he didn't then know that he was going to be banished for the rest of his days.

But why would you then not go back to reclaim him and allow him to join up with you again? If he took the hit for the team and you're the team leader, what would be the right decision for a real team leader to take?

I have said elsewhere in this book that it has to be you. You are the only one who can rescue him from his prison, and unless you do it, he will keep banging on the prison door, shouting to be let out, and generally disrupting your life.

So make that commitment now, not to ever abandon him again and to never again let him be disappointed with you. He deserves to have a happy childhood, and you could give this to him and, at the same time, open up a world of wonderful possibilities for yourself.

Step 6

Love

The Buddha said, "you can search the whole world over, and you will never find anyone more worthy of your love than yourself.

What then is the real change in all of the things I have shared with you today? Well, it is something that I've only hinted at until now. Let me start to unfold this step slowly, and maybe I can ask you to also read it - s l o w l y - In the most mindful way available to you.

Once you have done this reading and writing work, maybe you are ready to hear what I maybe should have said right at the beginning. But I made a conscious decision not to, in case I scared you off. So my sincere apologies for that, but I hope this gamble paid off because maybe you're in too deep now not to learn what I have hidden in what is nearly the end of the book. What I have hidden is a very precious thing, and people often do hide precious things for many reasons.

I am talking about **LOVE.**

Love is the fuel that is needed for the engine that will make all of it work. It is actually the fuel that makes everything work, but I'm in danger of drifting off somewhere else, so let's keep it focused.

When you have worked through all of the steps, and you've understood and gained some knowledge; when you've made solid contact with your inner child ; when you've made some discoveries about your history; when you've seen how you can be triggered and in what circumstances; when you've made the big commitment to yourself, then you are in need of love's help.

Love is what was lacking when your parents couldn't or wouldn't treat you lovingly; love is missing for so many people in so many ways. People are hurting, and this lack of love affects everyone greatly.

The love that we now need to find is the rarest love on earth. It is the love that we give to ourselves when we are in great need. We can act lovingly at times towards ourselves when we are happy, maybe when everything in life is going well, we feel good. We may sometimes say nice things to ourselves and think nicer thoughts about ourselves. But when the shit hits the fan and something goes wrong in our lives, we are upset, hurt, or triggered. We often abandon all approval, and love is nowhere to be seen. But this is the exact time that we need the comfort of our own arms, not their cold refusal.

Some of this is because of habit. Some because we were not loved well enough and we never learned to do it. Some were because we had introjected that toxic parent, or that our parents could never offer us, love. Some is about our own unworthiness; we simply didn't have enough self-esteem to think we were deserving of love.

But at the end of these steps, what is left in the here and now? You may have been loved carelessly. You may have been neglected? You may have suffered at the hands of cruel or evil parents? You may have been abandoned by anxious or addicted carers. You could have suffered so many small insults that then add up to great unhappiness. All or any of these events could be in your past.

But what is true remains true and as such, cannot be changed. This is a bitter pill for most people to swallow. If it can't be changed, what's the point of all this work? But what is left is one of the greatest gifts we possess and one of the most miraculous ways to change your experience, your life and your future.

When you focus your awareness onto your own inner experience, your own inner child (even if you still don't fully believe in this truth) I think I can honestly say that the lack of love that you feel for your self, is damaging to you. The faith that is needed to overcome a difficult, damaging or abusive childhood is a faith in **LOVE.**

So many hurt people want love, they often want it from a lover. They want it from their children. They want it from the parents of their childhood in wishing that they could have been different. It very rarely occurs to people to use the love that they already possess, the love that exists in their heart.

I think it is true that many people who have experienced difficulty of some kind in childhood have not always had access to loving others, they have often never experienced opening their own heart to someone else fully. Preferring instead to protect themselves and to build a barricade against the possibility of anyone causing them pain ever again.

So that is why we need to take leap of faith.

Why we have to take a risk, because everything we want is outside of our comfort zone.

Why courage is needed to attempt this heroic journey towards love.

All of the work you have done so far has been a preparation, a preparation for you to find even the smallest bit of true compassion for your self. Compassion is the greatest form of love and it is so needed for this task.

What is within our own power is to heal the child within you and therefore heal the person you are right now, the adult who is reading these words. If it sounds like a monumental task, it is.

But all human beings have access to this 'super power', that is the highest magic on this lonely planet and we call it LOVE.

Love is capable of changing anything, it can cut through anger, hatred or misery. With a heart that is open to love, the world can look like a very different place.

Almost everyone has experience the state of 'being in love' with someone, even if that love was unrequited, and it can cause a great shift in the physiology, the mind and heart. Allowing the person to be transported to a world where nothing matters, except the beloved. Where problems are easily solved, where altruism is shown, where forgiveness is possible.

But if the beloved goes away or stops being lovable to us, the world sinks back into ordinariness, into the mundane, the sparkle disappears and life can seem cold and difficult once more.

Self love though is the love that we never need to fear losing. Once we have understood the need and are committed to loving oneself unconditionally and continually. Offering patience, forgiveness, experiences of joy, attention, soothing, holding and ultimately loving. Our life changes, we are more open, more forgiving of others too, more gentle with ourselves and much happier than we ever thought possible.

Loving is made up of different components and if we struggle with the concept of love, we can break it down into acts of kindness to ourselves, acts that are possible.

We give our inner child space and attention.

We listen to the story of our inner child.

We never dismiss the hurt child's worth.

We stop our nastier self talk by knowing more about who they are and saying No.

We make a decision to be kind to ourselves.

We give ourselves gifts at every opportunity.

We reassure ourselves that all is well.

We take care of the physical side of life, health, finances, obsession, addictions, thought processes. All of these things can cause stress and stress is the enemy of love and safety.

We connect with others and find a support group where we can speak openly and honestly about our struggles.

We find a therapist, if this is needed.

We do anything that will help us to feel whole and loved.

It may sound difficult. It may be easier than you think. But whatever it sounds like, remember that for change to happen, something does need to be done.

Twelve

The end

"My soul is from elsewhere,

I am sure of that

and I intend to end up there."

Rumi (1207-1273)

I hope that you have enjoyed this little book as much as I have enjoyed its writing of it. For me, it has felt empowering to be able to stretch my brain to put all of the points that I wanted to say into a sequence that would not only make sense but be interesting enough to read.

I had been thinking about writing a book for many years, but as the old saying goes, everyone has a book inside of them, but not everyone will go through the struggle to get it out. I have sometimes found it difficult to write and add all of the necessary things for a book to flow, to read well, to make sense, to have a point, to have a purpose, to be relevant and consistent.

Don't even mention the things not to do! Don't be too repetitive, or even a bit boring, or not give enough information, or give too much. The greatest not to do is to deny the reader any hope that a solution may be possible.

Finally, there are the things about being a writer that can be a real turnoff to a reader. A writer can be too pompous; she can come across as knowing too much, and a writer can speak as if she is 'the one who knows' better. A writer can also use an inauthentic voice and not have the courage of her convictions.

It's a complete minefield, and if anyone reading this and decides to give it a go, I wish you all the luck in the world. But now I am at the end, and I breathe a huge sigh of relief. I'm glad that it's finished, and there is a huge relief of being able to stop the hard work and a great sense of satisfaction too.

Of course, the next part is also stressful, but it is completely outside of my power, for now, it is time to publish and send this little book out into the world. I have no idea how it will fare, what will happen to it, or how many people will read it. All of these events will continue without me doing much at all except watch as it hits a chord with readers or isn't well received at all. It is a bit like sending your child to school and hoping that the teachers like him, wondering if he will get along with the other kids or if he will be able to hold his own. Something that I was not very good at because it's about letting go and people with trauma are not generally good at this! But like every process I see within myself, I give it my best shot, and that's the biggest gift I have now; I try to adapt, I try to change, I sometimes let go easier than I once did, and I keep my heart as open as possible, especially towards myself.

It just remains for me to say thank you for reading my book. If you have enjoyed it, please let other people know what you liked or what you didn't like in a review because Amazon works through reviews, as we know.

Please like my author's page on Kindle and do keep in touch because, after a period of recovery, I might even do it again! It might be easier the second time around; who knows?

My email address is sueclancywriter@gmail.com if you would like to join my mailing list. Please send me a message, say hi, ask me anything, or just reach out for whatever you might need to know. I will do my best to respond in good time.

Thank you, dear reader.

Printed in Great Britain
by Amazon

17975298R00086